Praise for *Asunder* by Susan Wood

— Poetry

"Describing the grief of a woman in a photograph, Susan Wood writes: 'it was a wilderness/she didn't have a map for.' With the poems in *Asunder*, Wood gives us her own map for a variety of griefs, as well as pleasure. This is a wonderful book, full of intelligence, craft, and insight."

—Linda Pastan

"Multiple, dazzling, self-divided—*Asunder* is the work of a poet creating a deep ancestry for herself, a company of the known and the unknown, and thereby coming into her full powers, a fully realized achievement."

—Edward Hirsch

"Individually and collectively, the poems in *Asunder* are all the more beautiful for their continual reminder that beauty itself, poetry itself, all art, is an inadequate (though necessary) compensation for loss and suffering. On every page of this remarkable book, we see a sensibility that has been purified of triviality or self-display, struggling with ultimate concerns and questions in language that is at one and the same time lyrically intense and meditatively expansive, in language so canny, unfussy, self-aware, and dauntless in its pursuit of truth that it somehow heartens even as it breaks the heart."

—Alan Shapiro

"Susan Wood's poems are like fountains, or natural springs rising high above the ground, spraying jets and plumes of water into the air. They are both grand and veiled, powerful and soothing. But wait! Laced within some of the sweet, pure drops of water are poisons of the past and acids of the present. This balance of delight and pain is what makes *Asunder* fulfill its title and rise above the good into places of wonder."

—Cynthia Macdonald

PENGUIN BOOKS

ASUNDER

Susan Wood is the author of *Bazaar* and *Campo Santo*, which received the Lamont Prize from the Academy of American Poets and the Natalie Ornish Prize from the Texas Institute of Letters. She has received fellowships from the National Endowment for the Humanities, the Guggenheim Foundation, and the Fine Arts Work Center at Provincetown. Her poems have been published widely, have been awarded a Pushcart Prize and been included in *Best American Poetry 2000*. She is professor of English at Rice University in Houston.

The National Poetry Series

The National Poetry Series was established in 1978 to ensure the publication of five poetry books annually through participating publishers. Publication is funded by the late James A. Michener, the Copernicus Society of America, Edward J. Piszek, the Lannan Foundation, the National Endowment for the Arts, and the Tiny Tiger Foundation.

2000 Competition Winners

Jean Donnelly of Washington, D.C., *Anthem*
Chosen by Charles Bernstein, to be published by Sun & Moon Press

Susan Atefat Peckham of Michigan, *That Kind of Sleep*
Chosen by Victor Hernández Cruz, to be published by Coffee House Press

Spencer Short of Iowa, *Tremolo*
Chosen by Billy Collins, to be published by HarperCollins Publishers

Rebecca Wolff of New York, *Manderley*
Chosen by Robert Pinsky, to be published by University of Illinois Press

Susan Wood of Texas, *Asunder*
Chosen by Garrett Hongo, to be published by Penguin Books

asunder

SUSAN WOOD

Penguin Books

PENGUIN BOOKS
Published by the Penguin Group
Penguin Putnam Inc., 375 Hudson Street,
New York, New York 10014, U.S.A.
Penguin Books Ltd, 27 Wrights Lane,
London W8 5TZ, England
Penguin Books Australia Ltd, Ringwood,
Victoria, Australia
Penguin Books Canada Ltd, 10 Alcorn Avenue,
Toronto, Ontario, Canada M4V 3B2
Penguin Books (N.Z.) Ltd, 182–190 Wairau Road,
Auckland 10, New Zealand

Penguin Books Ltd, Registered Offices:
Harmondsworth, Middlesex, England

First published in Penguin Books 2001

1   3   5   7   9   10   8   6   4   2

Page 113 constitutes an extension of this copyright page.

ISBN 0 14 04.2434 2
CIP data available

Printed in the United States of America
Set in Futura Light
Designed by Soonyoung Kwon

To Letha Cole

The beauty of the world has two edges, one of laughter, one of anguish, cutting the heart asunder. —Virginia Woolf

Contents

asunder

I

Laundry

This morning she's there again, squatting like a squaw
by the trashcan next to the Stop-n-Go, next to the laundry
where I take our clothes, a whole soiled week's worth
stuffed into the king-size Ralph Lauren paisley pillowcases.
Nine A.M., July in Houston and it's ninety degrees already
and she's wearing a heavy gray sweatshirt, tattered jeans, her skin
the dark plum of pottery baked by the sun or brown with grime,
it's hard to tell which. Inside the laundry it's hotter still, steam
from the presses, the washers and dryers, swallowing the air,
and Maria takes the heavy sacks and heaves them onto the scale,
Maria, a Latina the size of a child, who speaks only a little English,
and next to her, her boss, who speaks even less, hovering around us
like a moth, a small Vietnamese whose knees almost scrape
the floor in deference, but not Maria, no, Maria half-asks, half-orders me,
"You not come back till tomorrow, okay, lady." Nine A.M., and on a TV
in the corner the talk shows are already on and America is airing
its dirty laundry, this morning a new one, "Liars," where a panel
of famous liars—John Wayne Bobbitt, Joey Buttafuoco, Tammy Faye
    Bakker—
try to judge if a man is lying when he tells his wife he's never ever
had an affair. Of course, he's lying, even to himself, believing his charm
will protect him, that she loves him so much she has to believe him.
How easy it is to lie to yourself, I think and walk back outside and see
the homeless woman still squatting there, how pretty she is, really,
wide gray eyes, the high cheekbones of Katharine Hepburn, dark hair
peaked with white like Susan Sontag's. "I wanted to ask you," she says
politely, "if you might have fifty cents," and her voice shocks me,
a mellifluous, cultured, educated voice, the voice of the upper middle
    class
to which my family aspired, and I want to give her everything, and I do,
everything I have on me, $2, and she looks up at me appraisingly,
I think, her gray eyes measuring the depth of my guilt.
All day I've thought about her, wondering what happened to her
to make her think she's worth only fifty cents, wondering why

she haunts me so much more than all the others I see every day,
the woman who wears her hair up like a Gibson girl and stalks
up and down the street in front of my high-rise in a black wool coat,
summer and winter, the old man, thin and bearded as the Prophet Elijah,
who lives on the esplanade on Montrose Boulevard, the black man
with a nest of dreadlocks who harangues customers outside Walgreen's
and calls down imprecations on the heads of the ungenerous,
the kid with a three-legged dog dressed up in a red bandana
who holds up his Will Work For Food sign to the passing Mercedes
and Jaguars of River Oaks. Is it because she's pretty—do good looks
    count
even among the homeless? Because she speaks a language
as familiar as breath? All day I've wondered what happened to her,
did a man fondle her in the dark of the movies—what a curious word
fondle, as though that touching meant to be fond of—and didn't anyone
listen? Did she have a husband and children and just walk away,
her closet empty as an open grave? Didn't anyone ever love her enough?
How easy it is to lie to yourself. Tomorrow, when I pick up the laundry
after psychoanalysis at three, I know everything will be
just the way I wanted it to be, all the tee-shirts and towels
and underwear folded exactly the way I asked Maria to fold them,
everything white, rinsed from memory, a heaven of laundry, all of it
an offering to the gods, the god of cleanliness, the god of fresh starts.

My Grandmother's Poems

Who will grieve for this woman? Does she not seem too insignificant for our concern? —Anna Akhmatova

They've disappeared now, as you did,
into the poor man's desert of West Texas,
river of dust, river of snakes, end

of the earth, the century's blood-red sun
going down in flames. They've disappeared
into the town's ruined, dirty streets, coyotes

circling the outskirts, their cries tolling the lost:
Sonora, a name incongruous
as the ditty Akhmatova heard in Moscow

the night they came for Mandelstam,
Kirsanov's ukulele plinking on and on
through the thin walls. This is *the real*,

not the calendar Twentieth Century,
what Akhmatova saw drawing near
over the legendary embankment.

Still, you're back there waving in the dark,
in the shadowy colors of imagination,
calling from so far away I can barely hear you.

What did you want to tell me? Home,
you're propped up in your screen-porch bed,
pen skimming across the page, poem

after poem filling the pages, white pages
that billow like sails filled with your breath.
What boat could carry you with so little wind?

. . .

Your daughter stands alone in the doorway,
though she will only dimly remember
this scene, will only imagine calling

"Good-bye! Good-bye!" as you sail off
down rivers of mourning. What was it
you were writing? Maybe it was nothing,

nothing a child could name, not poems
but scraps of Bible verses, the words
to sentimental songs, or maybe letters

to a "cousin" in "The San," memories
of the Saturday movie, everyone
in clean pajamas, the scent of aftershave,

his hand pressing against yours, time-bound
as the joking words you sang to "Ramona":
"Kimono, please meet when I walk down the hall."

If they were poems you wrote, they've disappeared
into rent houses on the edge of town,
into chilblains and heatstroke, into making do

and eking out, disappeared at last
into the stares of strangers, the boredom
of iron cots lined up like headstones

along the ward's blank walls, a pauper's field,
but today I saw your picture, the long face
so like my own, the hooded lids, and thought of her,

. . .

Akhmatova, how she struggled for breath,
lay all summer in a boarding house
in Tsarkoye Selo, alone, coughing

and taking her temperature. The year you died
her words piled up like discs of snow stacked
in the ruined, dirty streets of Leningrad,

but her silence was only temporary.
She would have understood what it was
you feared: not your own death, but a child's pain,

her grief, the wrenching sobs muffled
in a pillow. That's why you wrapped yourself
in sickness like a shroud, crossed your arms

against your chest, and turned your head away.
How that must have hurt you! And your daughter,
who said that because you knew you couldn't stay

you seemed already gone, a ghostly image
fading in the mirror's tarnished frame.
It's why Akhmatova wept for her son and stood

outside Krestky Prison writing "Requiem":
Not, not mine: it's somebody else's wound.
And maybe poems are no consolation

now, when the real century gasps for breath
and stumbles to its grave, or maybe it's myself
I'm thinking of, but, oh, I want you

. . .

to have had—something—poems, pleasures
of the flesh, a kiss, someone you loved
and hungered for, craved the way his body moved

over yours, the way his breath filled your lungs.
I used to think that after we are gone
there's nothing, simply nothing. But it's me

who's wandering by the porch again
and calling you by name. I'm out there
waving like a branch. Behind the frosted pane,

I see you dancing with Akhmatova,
two sunstruck tatters dancing in the mirror.

Diary

Memory is the diary that chronicles what never happened and couldn't have happened. —Oscar Wilde

Twenty years ago, a spring
   like this one, azaleas spilling
      over the lawns, the color of blood,

of hearts, of fire, a few the color
   of snow, of eggs, white as the blank
      pages of a diary. And our daughter

was like that, about to bloom,
   delicate, lovely as an azalea,
      a tiny bud in her red school uniform.

She was ready to burst
   into blossom that spring day
      we picked her up after school

and she couldn't wait to tell
   what she'd learned. This
      was knowledge and she thought

she was giving it to us, a gift,
   making a circle with her thumb
      and forefinger, poking another

finger through it. Do you know
   what this is, she said, do you, do you
      know what happens sometimes at night

when the woman is sleeping,
   that the man puts his penis inside her
      like this and that's how they get their eggs?

. . .

She thought it had nothing to do
    with us, and I tried to tell her, to say
        no, wait, it's not like that, not like that

at all, not the woman asleep,
    open, as though she were merely
        a receptacle, like a flower drinking in

pollen, that they both must
    desire it. But she sank back
        in her seat, she was satisfied

then, she didn't care.
    This was mystery, mystery
        explained. And all these years

later you still come to me
    in dreams and again I'm ready
        to receive you, ready again to make

another child as perfect
    as this one. In one dream
        we're flying, our naked bodies

winging through air
    and I believe that we'll crash
        but we don't. And every time

I believe I'm caught
    like a bee in a flower
        that closes around it or that

                . . .

it never happened at all,
    that I never did what I did,
        never left. And what does she

think now when she thinks
    of another day, the day when
        she opened the door of my closet

and found only the ghosts
    of my dresses, the shadows
        of my shoes dim as footprints

in the moist earth? It was
    winter then, gray and cold.
        Perhaps she thinks of me

then as someone who never
    lived, who never could have
        lived, a woman like a diary lying

open in the rain. Perhaps
    she thinks that this never
        happened, that it never could

have happened, that memory
    is only the blurred and fading images
        of ghosts, the echo of someone's footfall

on an empty stair, a cold pocket of air
    in a room, that this is mystery, a diary's
        ink-stained pages, ruined, indecipherable.

                    . . .

Now she is trying to write
    the story over, in her own hand,
        a diary of a life that has no room

for one like her. She is so like me
    sometimes I believe you had no part
        in her conception, and always I wonder

what she thinks now of that
    mystery, what she thinks when she
        opens and turns to the lover lying open

beside her. This is the life
    I would have had without her,
        and I envy her, I do, the red flower

of envy blooms in my chest, envy
    of mothers for daughters, the way
        my mother must have envied me too.

Of course, I haven't forgotten it,
    that first time we turned to each other
        in the long-ago dark and the night closed

around us, how much
    we wanted to make this child
        together, this blossom, this flower.

Geography

Summer afternoon, Henry James said,
the most beautiful words in the language.
It's what I think of when I think of summer afternoons

in California when the fog
swaggers in like a man with something
to hide. Sometimes he stays the night, sometimes

he's gone by dusk, the guilty lover who takes
his hands from a woman's face just in time
to get home for supper, though he's forgotten

the telltale signs, that he's left behind
a scarf, a glove, wisps of himself
for her to remember. Climbing a foggy hill

I thought the lover must be Japanese
he'd left such elegant drawings—a bridge,
the long hair of willows, a garden of black ink

traced on a lavender sky. He might have been
a lover I had once, a continent away. Each day
he'd face the red persimmon of the rising sun and dream

of home, though he went on making music
in his head. Each night he played a Chopin nocturne,
the passage where the music wavers like a face

mirrored in water and the composer sees,
just for a moment, his own death.
Think of Henry James in the Orient! That's how wrong

. . .

it felt to be apart from everything
he loved. It's what I feel sometimes when I think
of hills, who grew up in flat country.

I've been told, and believe, we carry inside us
a past we've never seen. I've never been
to Ireland, but sometimes, summer afternoons,

a girl stands on a hill above the harbor at Galway,
the emerald grass kissing the dewy hem of her skirt.
It is the nineteenth century and far away

she sees sailors loading crates of barley
on a ship. Here everyone is starving. Soon
she'll be going to America. A little in love

with her own recklessness, she imagines herself
on the deck, at night, in fog, a few possessions—
the rosary her mother gave her, a black-haired boy's

tortoiseshell comb—stuffed in her pockets,
wisps of themselves for her to remember,
everything before her facing home.

Photograph, Circa 1870

She stands off to one side, a wagon train crossing her brow.
There's a baby on her hip floating like a cloud,
a man and little boys clustered by the door.

I don't know who they are and from here the prairie grass
is so high that everyone gets lost.
Behind them, the house is sod, one cow moored

on the roof, grazing. Everyone looks embarrassed,
as if to be seen like this were no less
shameful than being naked. Outside the frame, surely

something happened. Why does she stand alone, I wonder?
The man is seated. I don't think the photographer
composed it, the picture's so unlike the century,

its more formal arrangements, a lit tableau
in which Father stands by Mother's chair. Perhaps shadow
and light were all he cared about when he focused

his lens. Consider where he was, after all,
that he must have appeared to them at first as a small
speck far off in the landscape, like a swarm of locusts

growing bigger and bigger. What brought him west,
what he was running from, or to, isn't what interests
me. Between the man and woman looms a space

I'll call a prairie. Like a prairie, it isn't empty,
though the white-hot sky, the ocean of grass endlessly
flooding the horizon can make you think the distance

. . .

15

is unbridgeable. Really, it's only a few feet,
though it seems like more. What remains unseen
there, her body angled slightly away from him?

If the photographer placed her with the others,
she must have walked away. Is she angry over
something, or is her stance habitual, between them

only resignation? It's her I'd construct
in the space where all the secrets are. Too abstract?
Well, here's the photograph. If I ran my fingers

over her face, the eyes deep in their sockets,
it might be a kind of Braille, like touching a locket's
inscription, the one my grandmother wore. I'd linger

over each raised letter ("DPH from WCM"), trace
their shapes with my thumb until something like a trance
led me inside the locket's mirror, each loved object

found, polished by memory's shine. Maybe I can read
the stranger's face in the photograph, translate her need
and pain. Not just imagine. Enter. Reflected

in her eyes, I'm looking out at me looking back
at her. Of course, we're not the same. The trick
is to connect and stay apart, two solitudes

communing. Here's where I'll start: Even as a child
she felt things, could be wounded easily. Sunlight
piercing the Ohio made her weep. Such a multitude

. . .

of passions! One chair with lion's head finials
came from her English grandmother, its wood familiar
as her babies' heads, dark thickets of curls she wound

around her fingers. The little girls died. A fever
took all three at once, though just what it was she never
knew. In Wheeling he'd promised her the world

and this was the world she got. Yes, she still has the chair.
See, it's the one in the picture, Albert sitting there
like the prince himself! Sometimes she's thought what a fool

she was, a bride trembling when he kissed her shoulder.
He dug the grave, one for all three coffins. Colder
that morning, by afternoon the snow began to fall

as if a baker in heaven had spilled a sack
of flour. Her mother would've said God's making a cake
to welcome His newest angels, but snow filled the grave

faster than Albert could shovel. The death of children
was common, but not to her: it was a wilderness
she didn't have a map for. Nights she'd sit up to grieve

without distraction, watching the sky, a few faint stars
pasted up like paper cutouts. Or she sat in the dark,
bird in a black cage, the night sky a cloth to block out

all the light. The blackness was absolute, immense,
and sitting there, the only one awake, she had the sense
that there was nothing else. The only thing she didn't doubt

. . .

were dreams. Once she dreamed she was a pitcher
of water. That was years before the picture,
when loneliness still stung like a bed of brambles

night after night and Albert told her he thought her heart
slammed shut with the coffins. But why did she stand apart
that day in the photograph? Funny, she isn't able

to remember, though she recalls what she dreamed
still. Her body brimmed with tears, a pitcher that seemed
about to overflow, so that when she opened

her mouth, an ocean poured out. *Like Niobe, all tears.*
Shakespeare, she thinks it is. She had her boys. Years
passed. And so, outside the frame, what happened?

The photograph, after all, was only a moment
in their lives: they were caught in its net for an instant
and then they weren't. Then Albert turned and said her name,

Martha, reached out his hand. Whatever had made her turn
away before, it didn't matter now. She was certain
she would've drowned in grief except for him. She'd come

to see that. Maybe it was distance I was looking for
and so that's what I found, mistook a gesture
for geometry. He simply stayed, pulled her back to

him again. She looked at him and smiled. What could she do?
She loved him. That seems important to remember.
The baby she held was Anna. It was September.

Her Father's Coat: Anna Freud, 1982

And take upon's the mystery of things
    As if we were God's spies. . . . —King Lear

It's Papa's coat she's wrapped in,
his old wool *Lodenmantel*, like a child

wrapped in a blanket of green leaves,
green as lindens raising their arms

over the little park just off the Ringstrasse.
They lost her there once. No, it was her *Kinderfrau—*

it was Josefine who got lost! Mama was watching Sophie.
This is not Vienna. This is Hampstead Heath,

where every afternoon promptly at three
Alice wheels her out to see the children

playing by the lily pond. Inside the *Lodenmantel*
she's a child again, tiny as Thumbelina

on her leafy pad. She's kept the coat embalmed
for more than forty years, cleaned and hanging

in her closet. You can't do that with a body.
It's hard to see who's here, really, though the light

cuts like a scalpel across the water's face.
There's Anna, Papa's little *Schwartzer Teufel*,

sailing a boat on the mirrored surface
of the pond, like the big one the children sailed in

the day when she was left behind. She bit her lip
and didn't cry. Her papa was so proud

                    . . .

he kissed her. He never kissed her.
Over there, some little girls are dancing in a ring.

Could it be Herr Professor's daughters—
Matilde, Sophie, and the baby, Anna?

Or maybe it's the aunts come back again,
back from the ovens of Treblinka,

back from Auschwitz and Theresienstadt.
Once the SS came and took her

in their big black car, but then she tricked them,
like Gretel in the fairy tale. *Come let's away to prison*:

We two alone. . . . But that's another story and stories
bleed and run, soupy as the English weather.

Everyone is gone now, all her relations. Everyone,
even Dorothy. Next to Papa she loved Dorothy best.

She didn't care what people said. In the hospital,
for next-of-kin she wrote "Jo-Fi," her chow.

She was only joking. Half-joking, anyway.
She's so small here, under the leaves.

She thinks she's lost in the forest and Papa
will never find her. Or she's the third sister,

a wish locked in a casket. Papa said
the third was Death and every man

. . .

must choose her. Now she's the only one left,
the youngest and the fairest, but all her words

are lame, hobbling like an old woman
leaning on a stick. She wants the dream back,

the one she had so long ago. Papa was wandering
through the hills, dressed in this very coat!

He wept because he missed her so. She wants
to tell him not to cry, she'll find him soon.

She burrows deeper in the coat and thinks
it covers her just like the swan covered Leda

with his great white wings. He was a god.
Surely this is the mystery of things.

The Sleepwalker

(After Edward Hirsch)

It isn't faith that leads the dreamer
from her warm nest, but a kind of fear,
the body ticking away like gold stars.

I know. Sometimes I want to leave the body,
to step out of it, blind, the way a woman
steps out of a thin dress and leaves it

pooled on the floor and doesn't look back.
It's an escape even Houdini
could never master, except in death.

And maybe that's what I want then, to die,
to leave behind a life that weighs me down
like chains anchoring a fabled magician,

to float again like a ghostly child
in a dark grotto, black as a night
without stars. But always the stars

keep on ticking, the heavy door slams
shut and I wake, astonished, locked
out but still in my body, fear still

a caged bird in my chest. And shame,
shame like a red caul that covers the face.
My sputtering heart knocks at the door.

I have to find my way back to the house
of the dreamer, the key that opens the door
of sleep, a lantern burning high

            . . .

in the window. I have to learn to lie
still, to love the dream of the body,
to wake, rinsed, in the lather of morning.

The Body of the Dream

It was evening and gold light fell
on the square, fell gold as coins
or the leaves of aspens in autumn, fell
on cobalt blue houses from a pink burnished sky.

The square was ancient, European.
I was with my mother and I wept
to be back in that strange, familiar place.
I'd been away so long. I thought

the light was the light in a painting
by Giotto, a fourteenth-century Florentine light.
But Giotto's subject wasn't gold light
falling on a village, but another kind

of light, Madonna Enthroned, her robe
that same astonishing blue, and on her lap
the Christ child, issue of her womb.
The womb a cave, a dark grotto

in which the child floats, suspended
in time. Grotto. Giotto. Was that the body
of the dream, was that what I wanted,
to dream that first body again?

And the dream changed, didn't it?
A woman appeared, a woman clothed
in a blue muumuu—that same blue
again—covering a body that festered

with sores. But she kept taking it off,
she wanted me to see. Her nakedness
was what I feared. Her pain, or mine.
And then someone handed me

24

. . .

a bill, my mother's charge for my life.
For every overcooked meal, the meat
congealing on the plate, each cotton dress
she sewed on her stuttering Singer,

every pinprick, even the puckering sleeves
I hated and refused to wear.
So it all comes due in the end, the fee
we're charged, and charge, for love, the price

we pay and pay. All our life together
in those dreams. But, oh, it's the first dream
I want back again, gold light rinsing
the blue houses, the body of the dream,

her body, body that never lived
except in a dream, the only body
we want, body we spend our lives
trying so hard to get back to.

de Kooning's Women

I've seen those paintings and I think he must hate women. Must hate
us. You say they aren't about us, our bodies or our tongues
or mouths, it's something else he's after, something larger. It's sex
that's scary. That terrifies. Devouring the other, the other
always devouring. Maybe that's true, and maybe it doesn't matter
who we are, with whom—whether the other is man or woman—

but it *feels* personal somehow to me, the way the woman's
splayed against the canvas, the way that she's dismembered. His hate
and fear keep him from seeing her wholly, as a woman—she's just matter
for a painting. That's why he's painted her all gaping mouth, red tongue
a slash, a slit—as if tongue and sex were one. Two breasts staring out
    like other
eyes—they're the Devouring Mother. And in the sculpture, too: the sex

of the bronze reclining figure is huge, engorged. Phallic. It isn't sex
at all the artist had in mind, the catalogue says, but a cartoon: images
    of Woman
in all of Western Art he wants to parody, a send-up of the icon others
made of her. de Kooning's not a misogynist, it says, he doesn't hate
women. He meant the paintings as a joke, for us to take them tongue-
in-cheek. Well, maybe the joke's on us. It's *not* ironic—that's what's
    the matter.

At least that's what I think. Could I be projecting my own self-hatred?
    A matter
for my shrink, I guess. The danger's both in being seen and not—sex
does terrify, its mess, its muck, a blur of bodies, swallowed tongues,
that obliterates the self, devours. But take the painting *Woman—
Red Hair, Large Mouth, Large Foot*, for example—it's everything I hate
and fear: the way he's made her disappear, effaced her. The other-

. . .

ness of it. Of her. Of me. And of course I know there's another
thing I haven't said—it's not what de Kooning thinks that really matters
to me. I don't want to feel desire like that. It feels annihilating, like hate,
this neediness and greed, this lust. *That's* cartoonish—too much like sex
in romance novels. So you think shame is a defense, the way a woman—
the way *I*—hide what I most fear, that I might lose myself? I'm tongue-

tied in your presence, I admit, but do you think *that's* why I'm tongue-
tied, or is it because of what you might think if I were to say all the other
things that I'm afraid to say? Well, okay, I'm not talking about "woman"—
it's myself I mean. In love—or sex—sometimes it's hard to be matter-
of-fact about this—I *am* afraid I'll disappear. The terror lies in that, that sex
blurs the outlines like the painting does. That's what we both desire and
    hate.

And sex teaches us another scary thing: that we can love and hate at
    once. Admit it, man
or woman, everyone's afraid of that. So what do we do now? Can we
    learn to speak in
tongues, no matter what we fear, learn to speak no other language but
    the body's?

Terrible Algebra

The Daughters of Edward Darley Boit, John Singer Sargent, 1882

Here, in Paris, in the cavernous apartment, vases
are bigger than children. Outside, the wind picks up.
The four daughters of Edward Boit cling
to the left side of the canvas, tiny Alices
locked in *une boîte.* (Clearly, they are waiting
for something, or someone. For something to be clear. As I am.)

And where is Papa, the missing *E.*?
Perhaps he is walking in the *Bois.*

But here, this is the wood of childhood, of fate
and fairy tale. Here is the wood of the family, retreat
in which we are most lost, apart. The room
tunnels into darkness, the open mouth
of the fireplace. The mirror reveals nothing.

Is this "a delightful view of a family
of charming children," as Papa's friend, Mr. James,
described it? Or is it "four corners and a void"?
The shape their bodies make is triangular.

In black and white, Florence and Jane, the oldest girls, whisper
in the shadows, like maids, or nuns.
Baby sits on the carpet, holding a doll between her legs.

But see, so far to the left, in a puddle of light, how
Mary Louisa, Mother's namesake, commands us,
takes in our gaze and turns it back,
cool, appraising, almost confrontational. Here is Beauty,
its typical blond curls. Her legs are slightly spread,
shoulders back, her red dress a stab of color,
like the red screen that slashes the right side

. . .

of the painting. In all the great *Annunciations*, the Virgin's
eyes are downcast or looking up, away, out of the frame,
fearfully, expectantly, waiting for the angel to come and fill her.
But this Mary is like the one
in Fillippo Lippi's *Coronation*, who looks back at us
in utter privacy, the frank stare of one
whose knowledge is complete.

Father, make me an instrument of Thy will

Outside this space, the wind
picks up. In the woods the chestnuts
raise their empty arms, waving good-bye, good-bye.
Mother is completely out of the picture.
None of them will ever marry.

And do I imagine that I know them now,
the daughters of Edward Boit?
This is guesswork, this summoning-into-being—
the way Sargent painted "from life,"
not drawing first but painting directly onto the canvas
so that it seems all surface.

But if, as Henry James also said,
each life has a terrible algebra of its own,
then what are x and y? Of course, they would be
different for each girl, but perhaps the artist
really painted only one Girl, from birth

to adolescence, disappearing further and further
into the shadows. What is in the painting
and what is outside it? If x is what I think it is,
then the outcome must be y.
But what if x is varied? What then?

. . .

What other values result in y?
Or perhaps y is always the same y in the end.
Maybe a life can only be understood
in retrospect, by working backwards.
Maybe not even then.

None of them will ever marry.
Florence and Jane will wander deeper and deeper
into the forest of madness. Mary Louisa will always be
the Beauty. Julia is the Baby.

Back home, in Boston, the four of them will live on
alone together, giving away at last the portrait
"in memory of our dear Papa."

Father, make me an instrument of Thy will

What are the limits to knowledge in this world?

II

Emily Dickinson in Love

When Sue walked in and saw them
there, her face flew up like a window shade,
then she quickly yanked it down. "They have not

any idea of morality," she told Mabel later.
She didn't say a word then, though, just turned
and left the room, just turned that ramrod back

and left. Emily lay back against him,
her *Salem*, her *Church*, her smooth, white cheek
pressed to his chest, her still lavish chestnut hair.

His hand cupping her breast. Oh, she wanted to,
wanted to go to sleep as if it were a country,
their country, suffered the anguish of letting him

leave her hungry. *You showed me the word*, she wrote.
She'd thought it would never happen and now that it had,
at fifty, she kept stalling for time, kept telling him,

"No" is the wildest word we consign to Language.
This was *a love so big it scares her, rushing among
her small heart*. But *idolatry* was what she feared,

the loss of Emily, that *Columnar Self*, real, erect.
Uncle Emily, she called herself. She stalled so long he died.
She said but little. Mourning—or *Election*—put on its white dress,

the way it had every day since her father died.
How like her father Judge Lord was!
A man who wore duty and common sense

. . .

like a frock coat and never took them off.
Still, unlike Father, he liked his jokes, his *Melody;*
it was overwork, an *Abstinence of Melody*

that killed him. But it would've killed him,
anyway, to see her die like that, that long,
slow death, the kidneys wasting day by day.

Bright's disease! What a funny name for sickness
so dark. *Little cousins—Called back,* that
was all, *and mourners go about the streets.*

They buried her in white, a coffin
gardened in grass and daisies. Vinnie put
two heliotropes inside, deep blue against the white,

for her "to take to Judge Lord." She was a bride
in white, not his, not Christ's, bride of the self's
struggle and shine, soul-shine, the coffin

carried through the meadow, May morning, light
jewelling the leaves, the apple trees, ineffable
blue sky, and the smell of apple blossoms filling

the day, a scent stronger than anyone remembered
there having been before, scent of apple blossoms
so sweet, so thick, it was almost overwhelming.

All the Way from Louisiana

This morning the smoke inexplicable
and thick as the past, the leaves of childhood
on fire and drifting over Houston. But
it's not that, no, somewhere in Louisiana

they're burning the salt marshes,
old wire grass flaming out to make way
for green shoots, a trick to fool geese
traveling south for the coming winter.

     Is a blue goose blue? Is a snow goose covered with snow?

Silly goose, those are questions
I might have asked once, but now
I think I know better. The smoke travels
all the way from Louisiana, the way

the past arrives from so far away
I thought it couldn't find me and years
fall away like leaves the yardman,
whose name was Butter, black

as the winter nights that would soon be
coming, raked into great piles and lit
in the gutter along the street where a child
lingered outside the clamorous windows

as long as she could and everywhere
the wet smoke of twilight bled
into evening, the sky stained red
as bedsheets or the color of leaves

     . . .

that lost October day. I was that child.
I knew then that darkness would fall
and I'd go in and they'd be there
still, their anger loud in the silence.

On the couch my father lying
like a fog-bound boat, his snores
deep in his throat, and my mother
nursing the drink she called a salty dog

that made me think of sailors
and oceans I read about in books,
their pages billowing around my bed
like waves. The children marooned

on the desert island have no one
to save them. But they're smart, know
which berries to eat and which
to pass by, know how to make fire

from two stones. High in a tree
they've built a house. What kind
of tree? Not the bois d'arc the leaves
come from, Noah's wood, wood

of the ark, wood to build a house
in which to dream we'll be saved,
two by two. No, they've built a house
from sticks they've gathered, a house

that looks out to sea. Even parents
can't find them. The story's over.
I lay in my bed, lay as stiff
as the gangplank that pirates

. . .

must walk, the darkness thick
as a night at sea without stars.
My father would find me, my nightgown
a flare of white smoke from the fire.

I was a child marooned alone
on that island. My sisters were dead.
Twice they'd bloomed blood-red
in the basin, plucked out like thorns.

Is a mother's love forever? Is a father's?

The child knows what she knows.
I was afraid of the dark, afraid
of the un-dark. I knew no one
would save me. In the fairy tale

Bluebeard's bride believed
she could look into the locked,
forbidden room and darkness
wouldn't overtake her, but knowledge

found her out and the key came off red
in her hands, her dress stained red
as leaves, stained red with blood
she couldn't wash away. It's fated:

the pirate will return and she,
of course, will die, just like the others.
It's what happens to a girl
who disobeys. But what if I rewrite

. . .

the story? Let's say she has two sisters
who can help her, that they've built
a pile of leaves, a pile high
as a tower. Where there's fire

there's smoke and someone will see it.
Look! They've summoned an army
to save them! Imagine fear drifting away
like smoke, how the bright flags of the future

appear on the horizon just in time.
Now imagine that future: maybe
anything could happen. Imagine hope,
shining like a light all around them.

Tenderness

I can hardly believe the story
they told, how he'd come home, exhausted,
in the sweltering dusk, the sun
tilting toward the end

of summer, and find us both
crying, hungry, and how he'd take me up
from the crib and walk me
back and forth across the apartment's

two small rooms, his shirt stuck
to his back, hungry himself,
while all the time my mother lay
weeping and rubbing her raw, red nipples,

until finally, long after dark, I'd fall asleep
on his shoulder and he'd lie down,
gently, on the bed, my body
cradled against his chest, my cheek

to his heart, a tiny boat
at rest, at last, on the lake of him.
I can believe, though, he'd thump my feet
to wake me to feed just when I'd fallen

asleep, if that's what it took,
like I believe all his life he lived
by the rules and never asked why,
or how, never asked anything, really,

except that the figures add up,
while he sat at the kitchen table
night after night, the adding machine
clicking away like needles, and under the table

. . .

the boy he used to be crouched
in the dark and waited for his father
to fall silent at last, save for the snores
that rattled his chest, and the boy

would rise then and go out in the dark
and the cold to find what bottles were left
and pour the liquid gold onto the ground.
Sometimes, though, I imagine he'd take one

by the neck and smash it and smash it
against the woodpile, crying and cursing, tears
and snot running into his mouth,
until he'd come back to himself, not sure

where he was, his fingers bloody with glass.
I can believe that. It's the tenderness
I can't believe. I don't know what changed,
but for years he never touched me

except in anger, never held my small face
in his hands and kissed me. Some nights
I'd watch the moon through the blinds
lay down a ladder of light on the floor

and I could almost see the burglar
who'd come creeping in, his face masked
like the mask I wore in the ether dream,
a tiger turning to pin points of light, tiger

. . .

burning bright as a sun.
I'd call out, then, for my father to come
and save me from whatever I feared.
And what was that, really? Not burglar,

not tiger, but something else, the self a planet
spinning out of control. It's the way I thought
I'd disappear in the cloud of his anger that time
he found me, down for a nap, drifting

and dreaming and touching myself,
and shouted and turned red in the face
and said I should be ashamed of myself.
Couldn't he see that I was?

Maybe he didn't believe in
his tenderness, either, and I know
I don't always know what to believe
anymore, but I know what I wanted,

and want: I want that tenderness
back, my cheek against my father's
heart, my small body circled in his arms.
I want it to be the moment night crosses

the threshold of day—oh, I want the sun
and the moon and the stars, all three, and my father
lifting me up to the window, whispering,
All this is yours.

Swamp

Once, at the bottom of summer,
we pushed on through the late afternoon
      heat that lay like a thick
sheet of glass over everything, the trees
      only a smoke screen

      for the scorching air. Exhausted,
we longed to turn back, but Caitlin wanted
      to see the alligators—she was two
and wouldn't take no for an answer. We came
      out of the stifling tunnel of trees

      into the swamp, the sun
pressing everything flat as a photograph,
      no life anywhere, not even
a ripple ruffling the dark hair of the water.
      Then the dog barked

      and ran to the swamp grass,
a smudge of gray ash in the fire. Calling him,
      we turned to go. Suddenly, she came
out of nowhere, came straight toward us, hissing
      and flashing a mouthful of swords,

      the heavy board of her tail beating
the air. Maybe her young were nearby and she
      only protected them, as any mother
would, but we didn't wonder, we scooped up
      the dog and the baby and ran as fast
                  . . .

and as far as we could down the path
where she wouldn't follow. The good news,
    you said, is that it won't eat you alive,
tearing the flesh from your bones so you feel
    every rip. Here's the bad news:

    that it will pull you like a lover
down to its lair on the mud-slick bottom,
    to have you and keep you
and eat you one sweet morsel at a time.
    We couldn't stop laughing,

    laughing because we were safe,
because Caitlin was safe, and the dog,
    all of us safe. We might be
limp and shaken and scared, but we were alive,
    that moment, there, in the shade,

    under the green scarves of the leaves.
That's the good news. And what's the bad news?
    We know, don't we, waking in the deep,
blank night, that something will come for us
    sooner or later, something will come

    out of nowhere, out of that swamp,
hissing and gaping, and this time it won't stop—
    nothing will stop its mud-black heart—
until it takes us with it, under, down to the dark,
    rank grave of the water.

Wishful Thinking

If every dream is a wish, then maybe the afterlife
is only what we long for. That's how it seemed to me,
anyway, a child, taught to believe we'd all rise up
and meet someday. We'd be with Jesus then
at the Pearly Gates, the mild, white Jesus at Gethsemane
painted on cardboard fans my grandmother waved
on summer Sundays. My mother's mean sister
feared not getting into heaven—that's why she lived
all her life with a drunk. I didn't think she had
a prayer. And I didn't believe we were all
"poor wretches" like the preacher said and I hated
the word, "wretch," which made me think of fevers
and a sour mouth. The gulf between the hymnal's
upbeat tunes and terrifying words loomed large
as the Gulf of Mexico. A woman I loved believed
we all come back in every life, a bird, a tree,
another her, another me. That's why she thought
the little red dog was mine before, the way
he leapt into my arms when we first met, and why
he liked to lay his head against my chest and gaze
so trustfully into my eyes, just mine. If I could choose,
I'd like to come back as a little red dog, someone
to plant raspberries on my chest and give me
hugs and kisses all day long, a warm body
to curl against each night and a plate of food
at the ready, and not just any food, but the food
I like best. A psychic told me I'd had more lives
than most, 4,002, she said, and she was precise
about that two. I didn't ask her what they were.
She was pretty and young and had an office
like a glossy magazine, and money. And it was
flattering to think I'd outlived many, reached
a higher plane each time. She was impressed
how hard I'd worked. We all have angels

in our hearts, she said, the ones we've loved
who've gone before us to the Other Side.
And it's comforting, I know, to believe my mother
is still my guide, that she frets and worries
the way she paced the kitchen years ago
and wrang her hands and cried. They know it now,
she said, how much we loved them, if they didn't
know it then. And a friend I loved, and failed,
who always answered *claro, claro*, her voice rising
on the sharp Andean air. The only thing she feared
was death. I'd like to think tonight she's looking down
and singing *claro, claro* still, the clear notes
ringing out across the broad, expansive gulf to where I sit,
here, where clouds and city lights block out the stars,
the yellow apple of the moon, and nothing's very clear.

False Spring

False spring erupts in February and everywhere the cherry
and pear trees burst open, pink and white as the skin
of the milkmaid in a painting by an old master. This spring,
these blossoms won't last any more than she did, doomed
by time. For now, though, they rain down on young lovers

strolling across the campus two by two, in full sun,
in sandals and shorts. Maybe they have a day, three days
at most, before something happens, before the chill rains
return, the wind, even the blossoms buried under snow.
Let them enjoy it. We were young lovers once,

with others. That's what we talk of today,
driving into the mountains you want to show me.
In the backseat your boys sleep, black hair slashing
across their round faces, so tired they couldn't stay awake
to eat the burgers and fries still unopened on their laps.

At home, your wife practices her expensive violin
and the notes pulled from her bow make the hollow
hum of your tires on the pavement. You tell me
you think it's over and ask what you should do.
Because I'm your friend, I want to answer,

want to offer some consolation, but all I can do
is wonder how much your children catch
beneath the slick, oily surface of their dreams.
I ask you what they've heard of your loud silences,
her angry shouts, and you say nothing, too pained

. . .

even to think of it. I know. I know I wanted
to believe that once, that my children could be
cocooned in sleep, oblivious inside their dreams.
One August, near the end, my husband and I
made a long day's drive, the air as thick between us

as my father's stale cigars, my mother's cigarettes,
those childhood car trips. I'd fallen in love
with someone else, he'd just found out. Feverish,
our son slept in the backseat, waking sometimes
only to vomit by the roadside. He must have

suffered in our silence, must have known everything
I thought he was too young to understand.
I wanted him to be protected. But parents
always think that they're protected, too, invisible
inside their envelopes of pain. When I was twelve,

we drove across the South, making a stop
at every battlefield. It was the war inside the car
that stank of old defeat. They thought I couldn't hear
and so I went somewhere inside my head they couldn't
follow. In the backseat I read *Tender Is the Night*

and touched myself beneath a cotton blanket and came.
I thought they didn't know, and it would be years before
I'd understand. Why are we such mysteries
to each other, all of us, husbands and wives, lovers,
children and parents, indecipherable even to ourselves?

. . .

The beauty of these mountains, the river cascading
beside the highway, seem somehow indistinguishable
from sorrow. You stop your litany just long enough
to show me where the trees have been stripped away,
leaving behind only a raw, v-shaped scar.

Soon, though, we've climbed to the snow line
and it's winter again, like a Christmas picture book,
all snow and cedar and spruce, until we get
to the place where it's the dark woods of fairy tales,
the ones about lost children, thousand-year-old trees

that block out all the light. Nearby's a place
you stayed once, alone, to write a chapter of a book,
an A-frame beside a river. You were happy there
and want to show me. When we leave the car, the boys
don't stir, their breaths like bubbles underwater.

Though it's growing dark now, we stand a long time
where you stood every afternoon and watched
for the same big trout that came each day to hide
in the place where the river makes a little cove,
waiting patiently for smaller fish to come

swimming by. He'd get them every time. Now
you're quiet, gazing far off into the trees, and I see
you have tears in your eyes. "It's broken," you say,
"There's no goodwill left. I just want to leave."
Driving back, you tell me there's no one else,

. . .

it's not that, you don't know how to say it. Once
you were young together, giving her a ride
home from college, but somehow nothing grew there.
Not nothing, just not enough. You don't quite
understand it, really, and ask me how I knew

to leave, as though if I could make sense of it,
then you could too. I don't know any more
than you do. I could say the selves we were
are not the selves that we become, that young love—
mine, yours, everyone's—is like this false spring,

fragile, impermanent, because it comes too soon.
But maybe that would be too simple. I could say
milkmaids, paintings, old masters, even love, even
you and I, are all alike, lost. And maybe words do
fail us, finally, maybe there's always more to say

than we can ever hope to tell, than we can ever know,
only this present moment, two friends talking
in a darkened car, trading stories they've made
from pain. It's not nothing. Sometimes it's even enough.
When you take me home, it's late and your children

sleep on, though their eyelids flutter and their mouths
are open, as if in astonishment, gaping, like fish.

Balloons

It was something I thought I'd never do,
be cut loose like that from all the ropes

of earth and float into the sky, but then
you told me not to be afraid and so

I followed you, one that I loved, my heart
in my throat, into the balloon's small space.

I was afraid to say how much I was afraid.
A wicker basket seemed the only thing

that separated us from death. But over Taos,
that autumn morning, the azure sky

bloomed out of season, a tropical garden
of balloons, alit with birds-of-paradise.

On the Sangre de Cristo, cottonwoods blazed
blood red, turning the mountains

the color of their name, and below us, a yard
of dogs barked and ran in circles, they were

so amazed to see us passing overhead. I forgot
to be afraid. It's like love, I thought, you have to

take it on faith, and so you just step in,
though you're scared still, your eyes are shut,

but you go into it anyway, blind, and then
you rise, together, on the air and soar

. . .

above the earth. You forget to be afraid.
That's how light you feel, how calm,

unbound from everything you were, the earth
shining so brightly from that distance.

In *Philadelphia*, Callas's voice soars, too, high
above the orchestra, a song of love and mourning.

"It was in that sorrow," she sings, "that love came
to me," and the dying man dances his IV

around the room, turning and turning until
the screen turns blood red. I saw that for him,

for many we knew, it was in love
that sorrow came. And I suppose it's true,

isn't it, for everyone, how love holds
sorrow in its hands, the way one holds

the face of the beloved and knows any moment
it can be loosed from earth, a face imprinted

on the clouds. When John's lover died,
his friends gathered on his lawn and said a prayer

or two and let a flock of white balloons,
white doves, fly from our hands, lifting

over us on the summer air. We watched
a long time until they disappeared

      . . .

into the bright blue ether of the afternoon.
"I know he saw them," John said.

I thought of you.
I thought how much I'd wanted to believe

whichever one of us went first,
the other's face would rise like that, a bird,

a cloud, a white balloon, a memory of the way
earth shone for a moment from that distance.

Loss

You hated that I lost everything you gave me.
First the silver filigree as delicate as an ear's shell
to mark my place in books, and the pen,

black and shiny, fat as a root, tools of my trade.
You believed that they might carry you
into the poem, that you might follow me

down long corridors of shade, ash trees
overarching the path to the gray house, away
from the house. You thought that I would lose you, too.

And loss hisses after me, insinuating, summoning me
from the corners of rooms where it's been hiding,
First the hard coal of the self they stamped out

as casually as one might trample embers
of a campfire by a river. Buried in a bed
of snow, my father slipped away down the icy walk,

the wishbone of his ankle snapping in two,
a clean break. Even my mother could not be
tethered to me, me to her. Even the hose snaking

into her throat couldn't hold her, and the oxygen tent
rose up in a cloud of smoke. A husband thick
as a brick wall. I lost two children, a girl, a boy,

stepping away from them over the scattered bodies
of men, corpses littering a battlefield. No, I lost
three: one flared for a moment in the stove's belly,

. . .

a tiny spark sucked up the chimney. And later,
the harbor where others might have anchored
abandoned to the white floor of the sea.

Words that taste like ashes in my mouth,
or a woman standing in a door, her red dress
going up in flames. If we were sinking, one raft

between us, whom would I lose? Could I make
a boat of myself to float to you? The answer lies
in losses heaped high as any house or bonfire,

high as a ladder that reaches a ninth-floor balcony
where I look out now over the flammable city,
over corridors of live oaks stacked like kindling

on the horizon, where dawn rises like steam
from the wet pavement or a breath caught in the throat
of winter, now streaked with red, now gray and cold.

Book of Days

Days turning over like leaves of a book,
"flip books" we called them, pages a child
could ruffle with her thumb to make a moving picture.

Fast forward, three seasons in a month.
First, heat pressing down from the mountains, ironing
the landscape, like Bessie bearing down hard

on my father's white shirts day after summer day,
ice tea sweating in her special glass, the scent
of starch and scorched cloth, fan a cicada

whirring in the corner. But in Colorado the stores
sold out of fans and so I lay stunned on my bed
in the long shadows of the afternoon reading

Freud's *Introductory Lectures: Solitude, too, has its dangers.*
And Thoreau: *What do we want most to dwell near to?*
It was the past I wanted to dwell near to, it I feared

and longed for: its mowed lawns and dusks, its soft laps.
And then one night the heat snapped like a wishbone—
it was that quick—or the way a child might snap

her fingers for the first time, surprising herself, thumb
to index finger, pleasure of that sound, pleasure
of mastery, and anything might happen. .

First fall of chill lathering the morning, coffee
and cigarettes on the back steps, the sky
an improbable Giotto blue, big-eared squirrel

. . .

astonished in the grass. How the light
slanted down, red-gold strands sweeping the ground.
A child in a yellow coat scuffled leaves in the gutter,

never looked back to where her mother stood
on the stoop watching. And through it all Pike's Peak
filled the horizon, shadows tousling its hair,

shading it, even as I looked, blue to purple
to black. Up there the aspens were just beginning
to turn, alchemy of silver to gold, bodies

shuddering in the early chill, the winter
coming on too soon, and at the top
a two-thousand-year-old pine, half dead, half alive,

let down its green tresses on one side, the other
a silvery skeleton, bare limbs raised in something
like supplication. So anyone, drowning,

might lift her arms to clutch the air. And now
this morning I woke to a cowl of clouds
on the mountains, snow caping the spruce tree,

sequined flakes scattered across the grass, stars
on a costume a mother might sew to dress
a Christmas angel. My prudent neighbor

had shrouded his garden, while I shivered, coatless
and unprepared. Far away, when I was a child,
we had to buy mittens the one time it snowed,

. . .

coasted down hills on cardboard sleds. Snowmen
melted by noon. All day I've been thinking about death.
Outside my window the cawing of crows

in the blue spruce, all day the chatter of magpies
on the wet grass, wing bands turquoise as a foreign sea.
Last month, driving here, alone, I clutched

the wheel, little silver coffin of a car thrumming
its tinny syllables against the road, and thousands
of lives whizzed by, all of them small, planed

like the landscape, mine smallest of all.
Horizon a flat line, a Kansas before and behind,
until the violet peaks surged into view.

They say, as they say, we're not
in Kansas anymore. They say a lot of things.
I know I'm going to die.

And what of you, old loves, old ghosts
like a prairie wind at my back? In love, Lacan says,
we give something we don't have to someone

who doesn't exist. It's what we have to do,
I guess. The past is a thin line from there to here.
Or a choked sob in the throat, like the one

a woman in a novel hears late at night,
in the dark, on the other side of the wall,
before she wakes up and discovers it's her own.

Strange Fruit

Here is the fruit for the crows to pluck,
For the rain to gather, for the wind to suck,
For the sun to rot, for the tree to drop,
Here is a strange and bitter crop.

I am listening to *Lady in Satin*, Columbia Records, 1958,
to that terrifying voice with so much death in it and it is
her birthday, April 7, and I am remembering myself,
1956, ten years old, up late for some reason, and there she is
on *The Tonight Show*. I have never heard of her, Billie Holiday,
this woman with a white gardenia in her hair, so sweet
I can smell it in the living room of a gray house
in Commerce, Texas, where I have already decided
that I hate the South, that the sign in front of the courthouse—
"The Blackest Land, The Whitest People"—is evil, that it isn't fair
that the maid has to sit in the back seat. I don't know how I know
this—it isn't something I hear at home—any more than I know why,
at seven or eight, I distrusted Richard Nixon. I'm not claiming any special
    virtue;
all through high school I watched the CBS News and wept
over the Freedom Riders, hated Bull Connor and his dogs, and never
did anything about it, never even told anyone. I never even had
a black friend until 1971, when I commuted from a bad marriage
fifteen miles every day with the gay black business teacher,
past the stares at filling stations to the town where that sign
stood by the courthouse. So what did I know that November night
when I first saw Billie Holiday on TV and heard her sing
"I Loves You, Porgy," her eyes cloudy as the day's low skies,
her voice with the sound of brandy in it, even more behind
the beat than usual, the rasp already a wounded growl?
I didn't know anything, but I knew enough not to forget it.
I didn't know about "Strange Fruit" then, how Abel Meerpol—
who would raise the Rosenbergs' boys, the Rosenbergs,
who I believed were innocent though Julius probably was not—
how he gave it to her and she was afraid of it, how she

didn't want it, though later she claimed to have written it herself,
and how the club owner made her sing it. How one winter night
in 1939 the girl Eleanora, who named herself Billie,
whom Pres named Lady Day, stood backstage at Cafe Society
and peered out at the audience, those white, middle-class
folks with *The New Masses* stuffed in their back pockets,
how her voice trembled as she began, then hardened,
those clear vowels with no Baltimore in them, gathered strength
until everyone in the room could see that black man dangling
from the poplar tree, could smell the sudden smell
of burning flesh, until that last word struck like a riding crop
on a bare back. How the room went silent for a long time
until someone clapped. And then everyone did.
That was sixty years ago and she was twenty years
away from death, from junk and jail and liver failure,
from the legend she'd continue to become. It's hard to say
whether she was brave or just foolish, a girl who liked
to get high and have a good time, an ignorant girl, really,
who left school when she was ten, the same age I was
when I saw her on TV, a girl who once swept floors
in a whorehouse, even turned a few tricks. I didn't know
anything when I sat, a child, in that warm living room
and saw her stand stock-still and sing every pain
she ever felt, and I don't know why I'm remembering that
tonight, more than forty years later, almost as many years
as she was alive. And of course in 1939 that girl
didn't know she would become her suffering,
that she'd go on to tell so many lies about the past
she wouldn't even know the truth. I know it's easy
to romanticize a life, someone else's or your own.
It's a good thing we can't see into the future, or we'd never
have one, someone might say. But I'd say fruit can also be

sweet, the peaches ripe on the tree. At least that's what I think
most nights, the way that girl waited nervously
for the applause to die out, for the band to strike the opening bars
of "Them There Eyes," and the joy, the *Satchmo*, in her voice
as she made one bumpy word from the first twelve—
I fell in love with you the first time I looked at you—

Lepidopteran

. . . I have been so fractured, so multiple and dazzling, stepping toward myself. . . . —Lynda Hull (1954–1994)

This morning a steady drizzle, forsythia
the color of a taxi in the rain that's come

to spirit you to some high-flying party, or the wings
of monarchs darting over the yard, a yard

overflowing with crab apple, double crab apple, pink
and white and rose, wisteria's purple, their blossoms

puffy, billowing, yards of tulle and chiffon to sew
your extravagant dresses. Reading your poems

here, their lapidary surfaces, I can't help thinking
what you'd make of this spendthrift season—

May, Provincetown, and after rain, sawing
and hammering sing all over town, each shop

getting a face-lift, new coats in spring colors.
Down Commercial Street, the Crown & Anchor

scaffolds over the harbor again, and overnight
the leather shop's disappeared in a garden

of pots and plates, blooming in every shade
of blossom. Transformation's what this town

does best, I think, just ask the drag queen
Marilyn—red lips traced in a familiar pout,

the beauty mark, blond wig, and she can forget,
for a while, every hurt she's ever felt, and so

. . .

can we who love that pretense, each thrilling
wiggle, the polished gesture that holds down

the billowing skirt. It's what we all want,
isn't it, to be other than the face we show

to the world, to be multiple and dazzling,
each possibility loosed from the magician's cape.

I've been reading Dickinson, too, who wrestled
speech in her father's house, wrestled

immortality, what she called *the Flood subject*,
in small, quiet rooms, rooms with their odors

of camphor and lilac water, of yeast, wrested
a self away from the expected good works, the cakes

and jams pressed into the hands of neighbors, damp
cloth on a fevered brow, salvation's jaspered towers.

Behind her bedroom windows, their traceries
of frost, she invented someone else: heretic,

poet, her white sustenance despair—
Mine—by the Right of the White Election!

But every girl loves a good makeover, you might
have said, and you did: the lush of red velvet

jacket, black beaded dress, those wigs
and silk turbans, everything that's *faux*

                    . . .

and glittery, what a friend once called
the intersection of glamour and trash.

And, oh, back then, the needle's delicate
tattoo, its sweet, transforming rush, and anything

was possible. What a will you must've had—
adamantine, I think, as hers in Amherst—

phoenixing you from the ashes of a life.
Or like a butterfly flushed from the scarf

of a two-bit magician to soar over the smoky
city, its barges and back alleys, the oily slick

of river, over junkies eclipsed in the broken
panes of abandoned houses, a barrage

of sirens mapping the future's stunned and lavish
avenues, its promises. And still the places

you haunted often haunted you. The past's
a voluminous cape, spangled and streaked

with grime, too heavy, sometimes, to wear.
But last night above the beach the constellations

wove their patterns of intricate lace, and low
in the sky the fat moon dangled like a psychic's

crystal ball, the one that hung above the shop
near Chinatown you visited so long ago.

. . .

Across the water moonlight spilled a path
of ghost money. Of all that group of friends,

I alone am left,
you said. Job's disbelieving statement,

its breathless, dazzled wonder: *And I alone
am returned to tell you.* And now you're gone.

Now you're a zinnia plucked from a purple
garden, the wind's whisper, shadow

of a wing stippled on the grass.
. . . *gay little entomology! Swift little*

*ornithology! Dancer, and floor,
and cadence, quite gathered away,*

*and I a phantom, to you a phantom,
rehearse the story!* Now you're gone, now

here again, back-lit by moonlight, a shower
of silver coins, *a butterfly extinguished in the sea.*

Analysis of the Rose as Sentimental Despair

(Cy Twombley, set of five paintings, 1985)

Here it is, the Impressionist garden
raised to another level of fluidity,
like late Monet, no shape assembling
itself in a wash of pink and red,

a watery garden where one color flows
into another, roses blazing and bleeding,
pink, crimson, carmine, scarlet,
until the color flames to blood,

the colours from his own heart,
and the heart, too, blazes and breaks
open, beauty giving way
to death, the eternal

in the ephemeral. No, not giving way
exactly, it's embedded in the bud, the vein.
Rose, oh sheer contradiction—
what made the poets weep whose words fly

like flags above the paintings.
Those early-waking grievers—Rumi,
Rilke, Leopardi—oh, how each of them loved his sadness.
. . . *his pains are delectable, his flames are like water.*

They were bereft without their pain.
And I am thinking now
of the women they could never quite love
(loving the Idea, but not the Thing itself),

loving the memory of rose petals
strewn across a bed, but not
the rumpled, semen-stained sheets.
I am thinking of Clara Westhoff

. . .

to Paula Becker: "I am so very housebound. . . .
a house that has to be built—and built
and built—and the whole world
stands there around me. And it will not let me go."

And I am also thinking
of my friend Larry Levis, a poet
who loved Rilke, who wrapped himself
in his despair, the way he might have

worn an old quilt all through
one Thanksgiving in Iowa City
when the heat didn't work. It would have
warmed and comforted him. That was long ago,

before betrayal, divorce, all the old
home remedies for pain—Marcia and Larry
were still together then, and I remember
envying them that. I don't remember

what we ate or what we talked about,
all three of us poets—poetry, probably,
instead of love—but I remember
the black lakes of his eyes, the eyes

of an old man even then,
though he was my age, not even forty,
the way he touched his moustache
and laughed ruefully at his own bad jokes.

. . .

I don't know what had wounded him.
About grief he was "enthusiastic, but wrong,"
as he said of his students' poems.
When we laughed, our breath

drew clouds in the air
above the rented dining room table.
But here, in these paintings, the clouds
are roses, clouds of them drifting

and spilling over in the rain, a lake
of roses, roses streaked with rain,
so many of them you can't tell
one from another. If to know beauty is to live

with loss, then why should we love
our grief so much? It's nothing special.
And if death is the extinguishing of all form,
as the painter sees, it is also the rose made new

again and again, as he also sees,
the way I once stood, lost
in my sorrow, in the shallows
of Deer Lake. Above me, the live oaks

reached out their arms the way a mother
might open her arms for her child
to step inside, and Cosmo barked and ran
back and forth across the narrow dam,

until he slipped and fell and came up
swimming. He had a look of such surprise
that he could stay afloat! And then
I raised my face to the place where the sun

. . .

stole through the dens
e heaven of leaves,
and for a moment—just one, though it was enough—
I was somewhere else, I was a body
composed almost wholly of light.

And Larry? Years later, he died.
His heart just blazed and burst
open. It was spring, maybe roses bloomed
beside the back steps of his house in Virginia.

It was days before anyone found him, his face
already beginning to disappear, like a drawing
slowly being erased around the edges.
Most of the time he'd been troubled,

I don't know why exactly—the lovelorn
vineyards of California? the poverty
of horses?—for no reason and many reasons,
maybe, and maybe just because he was himself,

a man who courted his despair, shyly,
tenderly, the way he courted women,
but he was sober, writing again,
and after he died his friend took the poems

and made a book of elegies, as all poems are,
a book I am holding right now. Once,
when he was young, he wrote a poem
set on the morning after his death.

. . .

My body is a white thing . . . now,
he wrote, *. . . and there is nothing*
left but these flies, polished
and swarming frankly in the sun.

What did his sorrow ever do for him?
It couldn't save him, any more than love could.
But that's not the point. What *is* the point?
To know death, to breathe deeply

of its aroma, to hold it close to the heart
as one might hold a rose, and still desire
to go on living, that is the human,
the remarkable thing. For a long time, he did.

Now he is water, rose petals
in an Impressionist garden, these rose petals
dashed to the ground, drifting and blowing
in the late spring rain.

III

The Unthought

The unthought is the highest gift that a thought can give —Martin Heidegger

When the weight fell and took the tip of my finger,
everything went suddenly far away, the clank
of the machines, the grunts and groans
of other exercisers, like a picture on television
with the sound turned off, though the bright room hummed
somehow, beneath the surface. For a minute it didn't even hurt.
The keypad they call it, but it wasn't key
really, just a small piece of me left behind
on the bloody floor, and I'd lost pieces
of myself before and those more essential to myself
—ovaries, uterus—not to mention the more metaphoric
losses, little shards of a broken heart, or the past
itself, which is all loss, its facts fading to dumb blankness.
It was the finger with which I gave the world
the finger, an irony not lost on me.
                         And later, someone would say
the most unique part of me was changed forever,
that my fingerprints would never be the same.
I could commit the perfect crime, they said.
And I thought of my friend's sister, whose fingers
                  all end at the knuckle—
But what were they anyway, those signs
of our uniqueness, those little whorls,
like snowflakes in which our selves appear?
Not selves, really,
but bodies, just something to tell one from another
until the world discovered DNA.
What *is* the self? It isn't at one's fingertips.

In the plastic surgeon's office, everywhere
I looked so many ways
to construct the self, but, really,
they were all the same.

In the waiting room, a brass Pegasus soared
over paintings of medieval princesses and mermaids,
and on a door a naked woman etched in glass let down her hair.
And the examining room hung with stalactites
like a cave, tables and chairs made out of rocks.
It was like being inside a fairy tale, and it was clever,
even, since what was desired was eternal youth,
though it was only my finger I wanted saved.
When the nurse came in, I saw
she'd stepped out of a painting I'd seen once
of Venice at Carnival, where everyone's disguised
as someone else. She had that look of fantasy—
golden hair below her waist, an alabaster face, and breasts
so large they had to hurt, but, really, she was the doctor's wife,
and I kept wondering if this was her fantasy, or his.

As for me, I was lost
in thought, imagining the self
as a kind of Venice, a maze
of intricate structures, solid and fragile at once.
First the shrouded, narrow Rio Terrà dei Assassini, the route
of murderers fleeing San Stéfano, pickpockets
hovering around us in their black cloaks like dark angels
in some Renaissance version of hell.
Or palaces of evil and the nightmare
chambers of the soul, the torturers
at 3 A.M., to which one passes on the Bridge of Sighs.
Then the sudden opening
into space and light and joy, birds wheeling
over San Marco while the orchestra at the Quadri
plays Cole Porter, and around the corner of the Piazzeta
the broad sweep of the lagoon.

74

                              Now the wide steps
of the Salute, its bridge of boats and candles, the Virgin
rising over the altar of the Frari in Titian's painting
or the reappearance of St. Mark's body, all containers
for the sacred. And the Ghetto Vecchio,
where the Serenissima herded its Jews, seat
                                        of courage and despair.
The self has room for all of these and more.

Sometimes the self is
                        other people, revenants
moving through the frescoed rooms like wind
in the chestnuts, curtains billowing
at the windows, leaving behind
traces of themselves, like a fine coat of salt
from the Lido, or the bright shine of time, its fluid patina.

The object of desire is to be fulfilled.

                        And that moment when
something reminds you—the play of light
on water, the shadows vines make, or maybe
it's some half-forgotten music, say a Mozart sonata
heard from the window of a house he once visited—
and the longing for someone you've lost
suddenly turns you inside out,
the body laid open
                        and driven into itself at once.

I used to believe
                    as one got older everything
became clearer, the self emerging
from the dark water, rising
to the surface, a limpid pool.

              But it's not like that.
Every year the waters
get muddier, too many motorboats
cluttering the canal, and the street signs
seem more and more confusing. Who would have known
San Zanipolo was really Santi Giovanni e Paolo?
You know how easy it is to get lost.
              Though that, too, can be a kind of happiness.

I've studied subjectivity. I know the unitary self
is an illusion. And yet sometimes
                    I believe
I can feel it, sitting somewhere
between my breast bone and my belly, not an organ
exactly, but a solid thing, fat
as a tome a child might sit on each night
to reach the table.
                 It's times like these I could swear
I've written it and I feel closer
      to death, to life.
But then the words begin
                    to waver and disappear
as though written in invisible ink,
      or water, and there's the shadow
of the unthought, a tiny figure
dressed in black—see it? there it is, just up ahead—
now vanishing inside Palazzo Labia,
now disappearing into the crowd outside San Stae.

76

Quattrocento

Inside the bus the strangled air, stuck windows, and then,
hours later it seems, we are delivered from our confinement
into the stunned, barren streets of Borgo San Sepolcro,
noon and no one anywhere, July heat blistering the stones,
smoldering the dust of the bus station. In the one open trattoria,

the only bad food in Italy, and on the TV, pinned high to the wall
like a TV in a hospital room, the image of an American movie star,
and in Italian we can't make out, we think we hear a word
that sounds like *crash*—maybe she'd dead, we think, though later
we'll discover, in the yellowing pages of a tabloid curled

in a Roman gutter, that she'd only given birth. Outside,
we emerge into the afternoon's conflagration to find the streets
still deserted as a blank-faced town in some science-fiction movie
from the fifties, a movie where something evil, unimaginable—
the Bomb, the Blob, the Thing—has vanished every sign of life.

But this is only Italy, siesta, months before jets scream
across the sky from Aviano to Belgrade, end of a century
in which we've managed, so far, not to blow the world away.
It could almost be the Quattrocento, so little seems changed
in the empty piazza, the same sunstruck stones, the same

shut eyes of the houses Piero saw every day, easy to imagine him
just a boy hidden in a shadowed corner of the blacksmith's shop,
damp curls bent over his drawing, the black mare's filigreed nostrils,
the way they flared when the metal seared her hoof. But here,
in the present, the *museo's* open at three, though today

. . .

we're the only customers. This is what we've come for,
our pilgrimage, stifling room giving way to stifling room
until at last here we are in his presence, hers,
Madonna della Misericordia, larger than life the Virgin
spreading her blue cloak—blue, color of mercy—to gather

the faithful inside, spreading her mercy everywhere, mercy enough
to envelop the whole world's misery, the Quattrocento must have thought.
Now, again, what I feel—here, everywhere—in the street,
sipping an aperitif at a table under the winged maples, or watching
an evening's passeggiata in the wine-gold summer light, walking

up the streets of Cortona, passing the houses with their little doors
for the plague dead, even strolling Venice's watery glamour,
touching piles of Fortuny silk, purses heaped in the colors
of every spent dream—everywhere, I feel in my ear the breath of all
who have vanished. Everywhere, the terrible lost present of the past.

Who was that girl who posed for the Virgin, the one
with the placid, lovely face who wore a cloak with its lining soft
as gray doves, a bunch of cabauchon rubies blooming at her throat?
The painter must have loved her, I think, he's painted her everywhere,
in every Virgin's face, in the sad face of Mary Magdalene, too,

though she's even lovelier there, more alive—Virgin or Whore,
it doesn't matter, she's still his beautiful ideal. I think
he must have forgiven her, whatever she did to him, betrayal
braided into obsession's silken chord. Who is the one kneeling
at the Virgin's feet, a child, no more than thirteen, a rich girl

. . .

in a high-waisted, long-trained gown, the height of fashion?
Bareheaded, she's still a virgin—so everyone thinks—
since long ago red-coated cardinals of the church decreed it:
because the angel appeared to Mary and whispered in her ear,
that delicate, pink shell—its labial folds and furls—must be the organ

through which the Christ Child was conceived; so woman's ears,
in modesty, must be ever after covered. And even now
the girl's father is out looking for a rich husband old enough
to tame her. Piero might have had her pose like that for hours, alone,
on her knees, on the cold stone, before he toppled her like a statue

falling in a garden, a flutter of goldfinches rising around them,
the scent of oranges and roses. And that man so sinister
behind the confraternity's black hood? Perhaps he is watching the girl,
her ripening breasts. Perhaps the painter means for him to represent
every secret desire we hide behind the mask of three A.M. It's hard to say.

But I wonder what desires candled in their eyes, brush-fired, burned out
in their hearts? Perhaps the plague passed through them, a lingering storm
blackening their skins, swelling their tongues. Maybe some enemy,
some Guelph or Ghibelline, rode down on their valley, torching
the village, flaming the burnished fields. Their sorrows were certain.

As here, in the museum's last room, in Piero's *Resurrection*,
where he must have seen salvation, I see Christ bursting from the tomb
as a figure sufficient unto himself, the overpowering body, the eyes
cold, arrogant even, eyes that don't see the soldiers asleep
at his feet, oblivious, ignorant of what has happened,

. . .

that the one they were sent to guard is free, that he will hide
his face from them, abandoning them to a future in which
they will surely die for allowing him to flee. One of the soldiers
is dreaming of his beloved, the way her thick black hair falls
across her face. What am I really mourning, time's patina washing

over everything, the past's weight heavier on my shoulders
than a plowman's yoke in some muddy Quattrocento field? What is it,
the vanished before me, the long line of the lost, or my own
inexplicable vanishing, my fifty-third year? Outside,
in the heat-stroked afternoon, the past is still lying everywhere,

even in the dusty patch of ground next to the bus station,
where the town's old men have clustered their fragile lawn chairs
to watch the passing scene. It's too late or too hot for them, and so
we occupy their chairs, waiting for the last bus to shuffle us
back across the hills to Arrezzo. It could be the Quattrocento now,

the procession that crosses in front of us, the priest swirling the dust
with his long skirts, a few men in shabby suits, the best they have,
bearing the coffin, and behind them a scraggly group of mourners,
looking neither left nor right as they walk slowly forward.
It could be the Quattrocento, except for the intersection,

which has come to a standstill, the little cars thrumming, dazed,
impatient to be on their way, dreaming of home, soccer
or a game show on TV, maybe a meal, a glass of red wine, perhaps
even a kiss, a lover's soft breath brushing an arm.
Even now, evening presses her cool cheek to the earth.

19 Pearl Street

What did you think, that joy was some slight thing? —Mark Doty

So this is your house—the model
Cape Cod, its clapboard white as pearls
a ship's captain might have brought back
from the Orient, shutters the color of ebony,

and at the window a snowy field of old lace
on which a family of rabbits scamper. The yard's
a tangled skein of shrubs and ivies
and a profusion of roses, their flushed

and blushing faces, heads nodding shyly
to strangers across the white picket fence,
the way Emily might've done in Amherst—
I can picture her here, delicately snipping

the blossoms, while in one corner a few
sunflowers stand watch, bright lamps lighting
the gray afternoon. But nobody's home
and the house must be lonesome without you,

though it's waiting quietly, contained
and dignified. If there are ghosts
here, leaving their dewy footprints
on the grass, they're not the kind who haunt,

they're just keeping it safe
for your return. They want you to be happy.
And, really, this is a house
made for that, the kind of house where,

if this were a movie, it would star
Jimmy Stewart and Donna Reed,
and at the end the camera would linger
over one last shot, pulling back

a little from the door to the gate to show
the fairy tale's enduring legend:
"And they lived happily ever after"
traced in perfect penmanship, arcing

over the roof like a half-moon, or the crook
of a sheltering arm. Oh, I know this house
has seen more than its share of sorrow—
as if there could be a fair share—

but walking by this rainy Labor Day,
I can believe in happy endings:
you two in the leading roles, two men
in love behind the foggy kitchen windows,

chatting while one of you makes dinner
and somewhere in the house two dogs, two cats
curl up in sleep. And why shouldn't we want
a happy ending, little engines of desire

that we are? Wanting is what makes us
human. It's how we survive, I think,
though sometimes I don't know
how you did it, losing the two you loved most

within months, while all around you it was
like Buenos Aires, like Santiago—the Disappeared,
your Disappeared, vanishing from the streets
every day. Keats would've called this suffering

. . .

"soul-making," I suppose, though there must be
other ways to gain a soul, and the final tally
of grief isn't a contest I'd care to win.
Who's had the most betrayals, the most deaths?

And who knows, exactly, why some go on,
even to joy, and others never will?
If you were here, I think you'd say,
"Loss isn't all we're given, all we can make

for ourselves. Just look around you"—
the rain-slick streets of Provincetown
flooded with tourists, men with new men
and girls holding hands, the middle-aged couples

amazed on Commercial Street, their arms full
of cameras and shopping bags. Some of them
have brought along their younger selves, their kids
with kids of their own in strollers or backpacks

or riding on shoulders. And look, in front
of the Portuguese Bakery, there's a whippet,
dressed up with a printed silk scarf, licking
an ice cream cone her owner—he's all leather

and hiking boots—holds out to her patiently.
Everyone's getting wet but no one seems to mind,
not even the drag queen Marilyn in sequins
and white chiffon who's pouting for the crowd.

It's all the costumes love can wear.
Each of us wants what everyone wants.
Above the thunder, music blares from a club
called, believe it or not, Stormy Harbor:

. . .

There ain't nothin' like the real thing, baby.
The boys inside are dancing, rescuing the afternoon.
In the middle of Commercial, two women splash
through puddles, stopping to kiss. They're wearing

tee-shirts from the AIDS support group auction,
and across their chests black characters trace
in delicate calligraphy the symbols for *KYUBI.*
It's Japanese for what persists: *the quest for beauty.*

26 Piazza Di Spagna

Was it a vision, or a waking dream?
Fled is that music:—do I wake or
sleep? —Keats

The day I walk there the sun
lies down in the streets of Rome and presses
his body against the stones and the stones
rise up in a fever, flushed
as the pink house where you died or your face
against the white pillow. (An image impossible
without you.) It's the hottest summer
in five hundred years, they say, and in Tuscany
the match-struck light ignites the fields,

fields so dry bats haunt the house
looking for water, and at dark Jim finds one
drinking from the bathroom sink where shirts
and underwear are soaking and screams and throws
it all, laundry and bat, out the third-floor window.
Later, we'll see it in the courtyard, stunned,
a poor broken thing, all accident, that won't die.
In Rome the Via Condotti is still deserted
after three, save for a few Japanese tourists—

the only ones who can pay the prices.
Even the trattoria whose bad food you tossed
from the second story has become Bulgari,
delicate morsels of diamonds and gold spread out
in the windows, while gypsies still beg in the piazza
and students gather by the boat-shaped fountain
like passengers at the rail of a sinking ship.
It's so hot today even the caribinieri have relented
and let them wade in. The way I'm wading

into this poem, lingering outside and hesitating
in the foyer—what is it I'm resisting
exactly? I'm trying to say something like leaves

on a tree, something about how it *feels*—you'd understand,
I think. Now I'm in the stifling library, where a scholar
holds forth in a corner, now Severn's room and history
arranged in glass cases, hanging back from going further,
deeper inside. And then I do, I go in.
I know you're dead and don't expect to find you there,

or the scent of violets and daisies, the same violets
scattered on your grave. And the light pouring in the window
so oiled it could be autumn, November, still warm and you
just arrived. In better days this might've been a room
where you could *sit and read all day like the picture*

of someone reading, a globe of goldfish
silvering on the windowsill. I didn't expect that—
to see you, your burning eyes, and your hands—hands
that always looked older than you were—clutching

the cornelian Fanny gave you and the last letter
you couldn't bear to read. *Shall I spoil my love
of gloom by writing an Ode to Darkness?*
you wrote once. She wouldn't disappoint you.
You might've seen her, later, in widows' weeds,
walking after dark on Hampstead Heath, the nightingale
singing from the hedgerow and moonlight
spilling across her path like a few poor pennies.
Even when she married, she never

stopped speaking of you. (Did you have time
to get used to that, when time was all you had
and you had none?) It's hard to see what good
would've come of it in any case—bills, and children,
and before you know it, there'd be tears
and recriminations, and poems still calling to you

from those same hedgerows. How hard to choose
between poetry and Fanny! Outside, the splash
of the fountain and the students' laughter buzzes

on the hot breeze like a cloud of bees and swarms
in the window. You're just about their age, a year older
than my son, still *a marvelous boy*, as you said of Chatterton.
And I'm old enough to be your mother. I didn't expect that,
nor the tears on my cheeks, though whether for you
or for both of us, it's hard to say. You were wrong—
in the end, you weren't forgotten. George prospered,
and your sister, your friends were loyal. Still,
the old rage bubbles up and the truth

tastes just as bitter as it ever did, the way your soul
had to be made again and again. More life! All you wanted
was more life—that's what everything wants—boys, bats,
every single living thing—even that posthumous life
your last weeks. It's always the same end
in the end, isn't it, each of us *mortal and there is still*
a heaven with its Stars above his head. (That's "heaven"
with a little "h," I see.) And the sound the heart makes
breaking is always the same sound.

Letter to Toru from Provincetown

Almost sunset at Herring Cove,
red sun bowing low
like the red sun of your country,
spilling a path of light
across the water. A bridge

from me to you or you to me?
I am looking west where you are
East beyond the round world's
flat horizon. At least I've heard that's
where you are, or were.

I am here where we were
young in our brutal innocence.
I am older now
and no longer remember the name
of our hotel: *Black Pearl, Plums, Sunset Hill*?

There was a man dying there
in those first days of the plague.
We could hear him dying
through the thin walls, his struggle
for breath. I didn't know
what was wrong, didn't know

how quickly they would come
to be familiar: the wounded
lesions, lungs flooding
their banks, the burned holes
where the eyes should be. The young
wearing the black clothes of the old.

Almost twenty years.

      . . .

Nor how easily
I could be cruel and call it
knowledge, how easily
I could break the promise
we pledged flesh to flesh and bone

to bone. *Finger-cutting promise,*

you said in Japanese, your finger
pressing mine like a knife.

And the faithless, what of them?
There were a thousand needles
they would swallow whole.

Where could you go?

There was nowhere you felt
at home then, no country,
no continent. Each night
the accompaniment of your grief

was Chopin—something in a minor key,
I remember, a nocturne perhaps—
and your eyes clouded over and lowered
with the falling music like black boughs
bearing their milky flowers.
Cherry blossoms in Kyoto.

Mine is a navigable sadness.
Briny, sharp, but clear-eyed
as the dawn that will follow
this evening's red sky.
Sailor's delight. Forgive me.

. . .

I remember so little of your language.

Hello   Please   Thank you   Good-bye

What is the word for *love?*

I would send it if I knew.

In the Venice Ghetto

Blessed shalt thou be when thou comest in, and blessed shalt thou be when thou goest out. —Deuteronomy 28:6

Venice, July, so hot it's white, glass
dome covering a glass city. Here,

in the Campo del Ghetto Nuovo, the poplars
in full leaf shimmer in the noonday sun

as though any minute they might explode
into flame, and for a minute I imagine they have, the ghetto

ablaze, blank-faced tenements burning and cries
rising like cries from the crematoria. But today it's still,

the campo bare, or almost—one elderly Orthodox man,
a pigeon and me. Standing here in the silence,

you'd never know what year it is
or that beyond these walls lies

a whole rococo city, an eighteenth-century courtesan
of a city reclining in lavish brocade. Even her name—

La Serenissima—rustles with glamour. But here,
in the world's first ghetto, it seems

Venice's opposite, the plain exteriors
hiding the temples, their arks of gold and silver,

the marble floors and delicately carved pews,
leaded windows looking out at the moon and stars,

according to the Law. I've come—
why have I come?—a non-Jew

. . .

drawn always to suffering, as if all losses
were equal, conceit that led me

at fifteen to imagine I might be Anne Frank
returned. A flair for self-dramatization.

Tsvetayeva says all poets are Jews. And maybe she's right,
maybe we are all standing out in the nineteenth-century

snow of a black Russian night
looking up at the palace's lit windows.

I'm not sure about that, I don't know,
but I do know one thing for certain, I know that

here, if I listen, I can hear the Lost Ones
weeping, walking the rickety stairs, the dark alleys.

Here are the heavy doors still crowned
with barbed wire and here the cast bronze plates

bearing their names. It was September 1943,
when the Germans arrived—there's where the mayor

put a bullet in his brain. And look, on the wall
is *The Last Train* that stops at the crossroads

at Auschwitz. Above the Scuola Levantina
there's a plaque to the old rabbi who tried to comfort

his people in the camp, and because I want to
remember him, I write his name, dates of birth and death

. . .

on a scrap of paper. There's nothing I can say. Later,
at lunch, *spaghetti alle vongole* beside the Grand Canal,

a German family sits next to me, the father hearty,
loud, doing all the talking. Perhaps he's kind,

a good man, I don't know, and maybe it isn't fair
that in his voice I hear soldiers' boots

echoing on the stones of the Canareggio. Shall I
do what they did, reduce everyone to a type?

I try to imagine this man as a little boy, a boy
sent by his mother to carry food to a family

of Jews hidden in the barn, try not to see a child
screaming "Jew! Jew!" at another child on a city street.

He aims a perfect glob of spit at the Star of David
pinned to her red coat, and the dying century conceals

its great mystery still. I listen as the German's voice
drones on and on, examine my scrap of paper again.

A gust of wind off the Grand Canal and the paper
rises and falls in the bright afternoon glare, a spark,

an ash—nothing can explain or excuse it,
but I am filled now with a strange kind of joy,

as if Adolfo Ottolenghi had escaped at last,
his name drifting away on the dark water.

Last Resort

I

This morning a cruise ship at rest
in the harbor, a great white whale
of a ship, launches ferrying
middle-aged couples from Toronto
and Cleveland, from Albany and Erie
to gawk in the free-wheeling streets

of Provincetown, last refuge
of the dispossessed. From where I am
I can see past it, clear out
to the trigger finger of land
where Long Point looms like the end
of the world and, beyond, the ruled

line of the horizon. The sun's
open palm comes down hard on the water,

and suddenly, as if for no reason,
in the middle of the mild blue
morning—no warning, no SOS—suddenly
I am thinking of those who are lost.

I am thinking of Viola Cook, a sea captain's wife,
who went mad on a two-year voyage to the Arctic:

no whales, just starvation and death,
an unnavigable sea, and still her husband
refused to turn back. She kept to her cabin,

silence seeping into her body's interior,
the dark spaces between bones,
until she became rigid as a block of ice.

· · ·

And of Anne Bradford, wife
of William, drowning herself in despair,
the *Mayflower* anchored off Provincetown.

No one seems to know why. Perhaps
there was no reason, no reason
she could've named.

If you'd stood then where I am now
you might have seen her
white cap bobbing on the water,
though you might've mistaken it

for the frothy top of a wave.
You wouldn't have known how the gale
muffled her cries, that everyone
thought what they heard was the wind.

Or perhaps there was silence.

No ripple of her on the surface.
As there was no ripple

to disturb the story, William's story,
a country, a continent.

Just an absence
at the center, the presence
of desire whose motion
is no-motion. Desire

whose air is silent.
Is cold. Is dark. Desire

          . . .

that says *no, no, I won't, no*
and will not and will not and will not

My mother understood how strong it is.
I understand. How much I wanted

to stay there, under the table, a child
crouching in the dark, wanted to hold
my breath, my ears stopped with my hands,
while all around me the boat listed
and rocked and rocked and rocked.

To stay there. Forever.
I will not and will not and will not

Now all these are lost, my mother
included, lost the way
everyone is, or will be. And still,

sometimes, I want to be
lost like that, days when the *how*
drifts away in the water, *why* caught
in an undertow. A mouthful of salt.

To go on.
Not just go on. More: to be
lifted, possessed, even, by joy,
like a breaching whale, his huge body
rising out of his element.

II

All week I've been worrying
this story, trying to make it

96

make sense. A boardwalk souvenir
to believe they're like us, a trinket
of reassurance. Still, I know
it's courage I'm trying to find here.

How to explain what current
keeps pulling that same right whale
back almost to shore, to explain why
three times in two months
he's had to be saved. Why tangled
in fishing lines, lobster pots caught
in his mouth, he was anchored upright
in the water, held fast as an abandoned pier.

I want to understand
such solitude, that vast ocean of loneliness, his own kind
dying out.

I want to understand
such sorrow, a great beached whale of sorrow
stranded in air.

This is my grief. Not his.
I know that. But what made him

trust them, those other mammals, made him
swallow his need and his fear as if faith
were his last resort? Made him
open that secret cave of a mouth
to her, one of his rescuers, and lie still
as a passive lover while she reached deep
inside the darkness to untangle
the lines from the baleens.

     . . .

And what of the woman?

Maybe when the creature dove down and away
from her at last, his flukes raised
in what looked like good-bye, she felt hope
enter her body as the vivid aquamarine

the whale seems when he rides just beneath
the water's surface. Maybe she knew then
the world is lit from within. She saw

that she could never go back
to the ordinary afternoon, with its mild, patient blue,
its bland sadnesses and common self-pities,
now that she had touched such otherness.

The Trick

The voice on the other end of the phone asks if I'm Susan Wood
and I say yes, and a man says in a voice I don't recognize,

"This is the Provincetown police and we'd like you to come down
and identify two bodies found at—" and I'm swaying, holding on

to the phone stand, I know what it means to have your heart
in your mouth, it's there, it feels like a plucked and skinned chicken

lodged in my throat and I know I am going to throw it up,
right now, I am going to vomit, but the voice goes on,

it says again, "Two bodies found at—" and then there's a laugh—
and I think, *He's laughing, why is he laughing?*—and the voice

changes, it sounds different now, almost familiar, "found at . . .
where are we, honey?" That's when I know it's L., and A., too,

in the background, answering, "The Sunset Inn," and suddenly
I am screaming into the phone, "That's not funny! That's not funny!"

I am furious and I am yelling, "Don't you ever do that again!"
I am furious because I have believed him, even for a minute

I believed him, furious because I've been tricked—I should've known,
he's done things like this before, tricked me before, but not like this,

nothing so serious, so awful—I believed him, I didn't even stop to ask
how the police would've known I'm their friend, would've known how

to reach me, I just, for a minute, believed him. And then I think of the others
I've known who've been tricked, how we're all, aren't we, tricked in
    the end:

. . .

finally she's home again, at last, after all those years in exile, she doesn't
      have
to be afraid of anything anymore, there are more books to be written,
      a house

at the beach, though something—she isn't sure what—doesn't feel right,
then the doctor points to the X-ray, the white spaces that are her body,

and says he's sorry; someone else wakes with a headache and gets up
      to go
to the kitchen, if she just has some coffee she'll feel better, and something

explodes in back of her eyes; another goes to sleep thinking of the poem
he'll finish tomorrow, he's happy he's sober, he turns over and pats his
      pillow,

he drifts off and never wakes up; a man is in the shower, he's lathering,
      maybe
even singing, this could be the night, because this one's the one, he's sure
      of it,

he's sure he'll love her forever and ever, and then his heart tightens,
it just bursts, it can't contain all this happiness, can't contain all these
      years,

it can't, finally, contain *him*, and the last thing he sees, the very last thing
he sees, is a cliff of white tile, he didn't know it could be that white,

and the water spiraling and spiraling down the drain.
What did they think? Did they think they were going to live forever?

In Cortona, Thinking of Bill

—William Matthews (1942–1997)

No wonder you loved this country, place
of civility and pleasure—you were a connoisseur
of both, those stays against the poet's sickness:
a strain of terminal sadness. It could kill us all
in the end, I guess, though you wanted to deny it
in the worst way. And how bad was that?
Let me count the ways you dressed up
your grief: music, especially jazz, and basketball
—all sports, in fact—and poems, of course, and food
and wine, and travel anywhere. Don't forget marriage,
that most confusing stay against confusion yet—
you tried three times, officially, and more. And always,
always wit—too glib sometimes, I thought,
and you agreed—but a mind sharpening
and sharpening its knives. It was your heart,

though, that brought you down in a cloud
of smoke, like Auden's making "a last fist"
and fighting back, punching your lights out,
while water meant to revive you after a long day
swirled over the bathroom tiles, sluiced down the drain.
Your coat lying on the bed and opera tickets in the pocket
—I don't know, but I like to imagine it was *Turandot*,
the opera Puccini left unfinished at his death,
though there was no *dimenuendo* of his powers.
Or maybe *Tosca*: the tenor—he's an artist—
about to die, singing "E lucevan le stelle," and then
reprieve, and oh, the joy, the reunion with his love!
But no, it's all a cruel trick—the guns
have bullets in them. These are ironies

you'd have appreciated, I think, taking the long view,
like this one, for instance, from the terrace at Tonino's,

the whole Valdichiana coming to light. Lake Trasimeno,
far off, a silver cup on a silver plate, and on the blue hills,
sunflowers winking on like millions of lamps. And the light
itself, liquid, gold, oil poured from an olive grove.
This morning I've been reading your book,
the posthumous one—how hard it is to say that.
You didn't believe that "Auden died
because his face invaded his body," as someone said,
that the best suffer most and it shows, but here you are
looking out from your book, your face in its gravity
longer than shadows on the wall behind you,
bags under your eyes deep enough to hold a world
of tears. I can hear you giggle at that—
you had a nose for self-pity, especially your own—
it stank to high heaven. It's not suffering
that eats us, you said, but our own bad habits.

Later, I'll walk home slowly up the steep hill
by the peach-colored hospital, the day already gone
slack with heat, home to the lax hours of books and naps.
Then evening, with its passeggiata, the already familiar
faces filling the piazza, while in front of Bar Signorelli
the town's rich widows gossip at their favorite table,
nursing Campari and sodas and comparing their lovers—
young men from the country said to visit late at night
when all the town's asleep. Such civility and pleasure!
And then, the swallows diving and swooping
over the piazza at dusk, or hovering over
the tall houses, the ones with the small, second doors
only the dead can pass through. Those birds remind me
of angels in Luca Signorelli's *Nativity*—Luca,
local boy made good—angels hovering over the body
of a tiny, oddly ancient Christ Child. At night

they gather on the roof of the hospital—
Santa Maria della Misericordia, Saint Mary of Mercy.
How much you loved what words do, and defy,
and how close they are, our suffering
and what saves us.

Chekhov

In a movie I saw once, the actors were playing actors in a play by
    Chekhov,
The Three Sisters. In the play someone asked Masha, the married
    sister, why
she always wore black, and she said, "Because I'm in mourning for my
    life."

I couldn't find those lines in the translation I have—I've read it twice—and
    maybe
it's just the difference in translations or maybe the actors improvised the
    lines,
but I think if Chekhov didn't write them he should have. *I'm in mourning for
    my life.*

That's what it's felt like to be me sometimes. A lot of the time, really.
And I thought how the characters in Chekhov are always sad and full of
    longing.
They're nostalgic for the past and don't want anything to change, and yet

the world they've known has always disappeared, or is about to. It's true
that sometimes they seem foolish, like Masha and her sisters when they
    talk
about going back to Moscow, which you, the audience, know is not
    at all

what they remember it to be, and, besides, they're never really going
    back there.
But I thought, too, how, even when they're foolish, they're often brave.
Like Masha saying at the play's end, "We must live," or her sister Olga
    insisting

that "Our lives aren't over," that soon "we'll find out why we live, why we
    suffer."

They're never going to go to Moscow, Masha's husband is a bore and
    her lover's
left her, Olga will always be alone, the headmistress of a provincial
    school, and still

they want to live and find meaning in it. I suppose you could see them as
    desperate
or pathetic, willfully blind, or brave, depending on your mood. Today I
    didn't feel
brave, particularly, but more like Vershinin, Masha's lover, when he says
    that

everyone will forget them when they die, that maybe life means nothing. It
    rained
all day, the rain hitting against the windows like sticks, and wind shook
    the whole house.
I went for a walk at Race Point Beach and watched the waves tossed
    around as if

they were being beaten, the wind slapping the sand again and again. (In
    literature
this is called "mimetic strategy": the weather imitating the characters'
    moods, like the storm
at the end of *The Sea Gull*.) I stood for a long time staring out at the
    horizon—

it looked as if someone drew it with a ruler, that the world really is flat
    and when you
got there, you'd just fall off—and thought about my life. About my
    marriage, my lovers,
and how I'd always chosen people who couldn't love me, whom I
    couldn't love.

. . .

105

About how much I'd hurt my children. I thought about people I've loved
who've died
or been lost in other ways to me and how much I missed them. But mostly
I thought that
my life is more than half over, two-thirds over maybe, that I haven't done
as much

as I'd intended to, and maybe never will. That maybe I'd always be
alone, that someday
it might be as though I'd never lived. Saying it like this, condensed, I
sound childish and
self-pitying—laughable, really—but it *seemed* deeper at the time, though I
suppose it

always does to the one who's sad: I felt sad all the way up and down my
body—my bones
were sad, my blood was sad, every cell in me was sad. Like a character
in Chekhov.
Then I went back to the apartment where I was staying and my friend
Marie came over.

She wanted to drive my car because she's thinking about getting one like
it, so I said sure
and we went driving along the bay toward Truro for a while, the tires and
windshield
wipers going "whoosh, whoosh, whoosh" in the rain. And later we went
to dinner

at the Dancing Lobster, a name that makes me laugh and think of Lewis
Carroll,
whom some would call a pervert, but I think he was just a lonely man
who loved beauty
and delight—he didn't want to *do* anything with it, he just wanted to look
at it and be

106

. . .

near it. We sat in the back so we could see the water, the lights coming
   on in the harbor,
and I had a perfect little tagliatelle with shrimp and tomatoes and fresh
   basil and garlic
and with it an Oregon pinot noir. We talked a while about poetry and
   poets and about

the halcyon days in Cambridge in the early eighties when all the poets
   knew and liked
each other and talked poetry all day and night, a little like Russia in the
   nineteenth century,
or the sisters' Moscow, anyway. I was laughing, and Marie said, "Look at
   you, you look

like you're fifteen years old!" I don't, of course, but I liked it that she said
   that. I gave her
my book and she gave me hers and we talked about our pasts and our
   regrets, all we'd lost,
about her brother John dying and how, after he died, she couldn't write
   but sat at her desk

staring all day at a blank sheet of paper. All she could think of to say
   was, "John is dead,"
and the next day, "John is still dead." And then after a while she began to
   write again,
those brave and terrifying poems that cut and heal—they bleed you and
   you feel better.

She went on living. When we went outside the rain had stopped, it was
   cooler and the sky
was "all diamonds," as Chekhov once said. The night still smelled like
   rain and sea and
salt. In the harbor a ship's horn cried *I want I want I want*, and out there
   somewhere

. . .

in the dark, I knew, were the ocean and the whale rescued for the third
    time in the harbor
last week, the whale who was so insistent on living; there were snowy
    hills of dunes and
the pale violet flowers of sea lavender, and in the woods at Pilgrim
    Heights among the oaks

and copper beech I could find again the single apple tree, a last re-
    minder of a farm and
the lives that were once lived there. Then Marie asked me if I thought that
    I might want
to sublet her apartment in Provincetown in the winter and early spring,
    and I thought, no,

I can't possibly do that, and then I thought, why not? Why not do the
    unexpected thing,
something I hadn't planned? Why not surprise myself for once? When I
    got back to
the apartment, the heat had been fixed, so I turned it up and put on my
    gray wool socks,

made to be warm at forty below, and the bathrobe I love, the one with
    the blue and red
and yellow cups and saucers sprinkled all over it, and I worked on a
    poem for a while,
a poem I like. Then I got into bed and read Marie's book and thought,
    "Yes, this is what

the living do." I don't know why we suffer. Maybe I never will. Maybe I'll
    never go to
Moscow, *my* Moscow, but I can go to Provincetown again, or to Italy and
    the blue hills
gold-dusted with sunflowers, their light poured back into the sky. I can go
    there.

Desire's Kimono

Whatever we do, the self
     goes on spinning desire
          from deep inside, the self

     a silkworm spinning out its various forms,
enough silk to fill the world's warehouse with yearning!
     And from that fabric, kimonos are made

         in all the forms desire can take.
     Here are the chaste and delicate wishes,
kimonos fragile as the one my friend found once,

     hanging on the back wall of an import shop, clinging
         there like a moth disguising itself
     as a shadow of pale winter light.

And here are the insistent longings, the ones that interest me
     most, though small desires, too, have their own designs on us.
         The large ones are fevered, swooning, burning

     from the inside out. Fabric of darkness, of liquid, fabric
of the body's secret grottos, spun into kimonos to clothe
     the favorite courtesan. Only she may wear them,

         the story says, and she may wear them only.
     Their colors are the red of painted lips, of menstrual blood,
black of hair unbound in ropes of ebony, black of night, deepest night

     in which the lover comes. And on them is embroidered
         every attitude the body can devise, lovers shown
     in every form and pose of love. Lip and tongue and breast.

             . . .

A manual for pleasure. So that when she moves
      the lovers move, their bodies shifting
            with each rustle of the silk, limb to limb

      and mouth to mouth, first one on top, then one
behind, below, kisses here and here and here.
      And seeing this, she is riven

            with desire and so enflamed
      that she is drenched with love
and must lie silent and unmoving on her silken bed

      or else she'll drown. Until at last her lover comes
            at midnight to her room and lights the lamp
      and takes down the kimono from her shoulders.

Each night they must enact this ritual. Possessed
      by beauty, her desire strung tight as invisible wires
            to bind her to the bed, she sees, closing her eyes,

      only their bodies mirroring the bodies
on the robe, feels in dreams his body moving over hers,
      silk crackling like the cracking open of a shell.

            And the lover, too, dreaming of beauty, dreams
      the falling open of desire, feels their bodies move
like rivers in their hands, the way love pools in the deepest lake.

      This is a story of pleasure and of pain. This is a story
            with no end. We wrap ourselves in longing
      and lie down. We rise. We begin again.

Notes

"My Grandmother's Poems": The last seven lines are an adaptation of Anna Akhmatova's "March Elegy."

"The Sleepwalker" is a response to Edward Hirsch's poem "For the Sleepwalkers."

"Terrible Algebra" is indebted to Adam Gopnik, "Sargent's Pearls," *The New Yorker*, February 15, 1999, and to David Lubin, *Act of Portrayal: Eakins, Sargent, James*, Yale, 1985.

"Emily Dickinson in Love" draws on Cynthia Griffin Wolff's excellent critical biography, *Emily Dickinson* (Addison-Wesley, 1988). The italicized phrases are quoted from Dickinson's letters.

"Swamp" is for Peter, Jill, and Caitlin Brown.

"Wishful Thinking" is in memory of Mercedes Valdivieso.

"Lepidopteran" remembers Lynda Hull (1954–1994) and makes reference to her poems and to the poems and letters of Emily Dickinson.

"Analysis of the Rose as Sentimental Despair" is in memory of Larry Levis (1946–1996). This series of five paintings by Cy Twombley hangs in the Twombley Gallery of the Menil Museum in Houston. At the top of the paintings are quotations from the poets Rumi, Rilke, and Leopardi. The artist Clara Westhoff was Rilke's wife and the artist Paula Becker was their friend, in memory of whom Rilke wrote "Requiem." The italicized lines in stanza 27 are from Larry's poem "The Morning After My Death" in his second book, *The Afterlife*.

"The Unthought": the idea of "self" as expressing the highest degree of Heidegger's concept of the unthought was suggested by Christopher Bollas in *Cracking Up: The Work of Unconscious Experience*, Hill and Wang, 1995.

"Quattrocento": Borgo San Sepolcro is a Tuscan town that was the birthplace of Piero della Francesca. Its Museo Civico houses two of his masterpieces, the *Madonna della Misercordia* and the *Resurrection*.

"19 Pearl Street" is for Mark Doty and Paul Lisicky.

"26 Piazza di Spagna" is the address of the house in Rome where John Keats died on February 23, 1820. It is now preserved as a museum, the Keats-Shelley Memorial House.

"The Trick" is for Ann Beattie and Lincoln Perry.

"In Cortona, Thinking of Bill" is in memory of William Matthews (1942–1997), and the phrases in quotation marks in the second and third stanzas are from his poem "In Memory of W. H. Auden."

"Chekhov" is for Marie Howe.

Acknowledgments

Grateful acknowledgement is made to the editors of the following journals in which some of these poems appeared, sometimes in slightly different form:

Antioch Review: "False Spring"
Columbia: A Journal of Poetry and Prose: "Emily Dickinson in Love," "Book of Days"
DoubleTake: "Photograph, Circa 1870"
The Gettysburg Review: "My Grandmother's Poems," "Diary," "The Body of the Dream," "The Trick"
New England Review: "Letter to Toru from Provincetown"
The Paris Review: "Geography," "Swamp," "de Kooning's Women," "Her Father's Coat: Anna Freud, 1982," "Terrible Algebra"
Ploughshares: "Analysis of the Rose as Sentimental Despair"
Smartish Pace: "Tenderness"
The Southern Review: "All the Way from Louisiana"
TriQuarterly: "Desire's Kimono," "The Unthought"
Western Humanities Review: "Loss"
Witness: "19 Pearl Street," "Balloons"
"Laundry" appeared in *Roundup: An Anthology of Texas Poets from 1973 to 1998,* edited and introduced by Tom Oliphant, Prickly Pear Press, 1999.
"Diary" appeared in *The Pushcart Prize 2000 XXIV: Best of the Small Presses,* edited by Bill Henderson with the Pushcart Prize editors, Pushcart Press, 1999.
"Analysis of the Rose as Sentimental Despair" appeared in *The Best American Poetry 2000,* Rita Dove, editor, and David Lehman, series editor, Scribner's, 2000.

II would like to thank the John Simon Guggenheim Foundation for its generous fellowship, which enabled me to finish this book, the Fine Arts Work Center in Provincetown for a Senior Writer's Fellowship, and Colorado College for the time I spent there as the John Ebey Visiting Writer. As always, I am grateful to Rice University for sabbaticals and summer research grants and for supplementing my Guggenheim Fellowship so that I could take additional time off to write. And, of course, special thanks to Garrett Hongo for selecting *Asunder* for the National Poetry Series. To Welynda Wright for introducing me to Italy. To my poet friends, many of whom read these poems in manuscript and were generous with their help and support, both personally and professionally. To Marsha Recknagel, the kind of friend everyone should be lucky enough to have. And, above all, to Caitlin and Caleb Wood, who mean everything to me.